Dorothea Ruggles-Brise

The Edinburgh Syren

Or, musical bouquet; being a new selection of modern songs, sung at the various

places of amusement in Great Britain and Ireland

Dorothea Ruggles-Brise

The Edinburgh Syren
Or, musical bouquet; being a new selection of modern songs, sung at the various places of amusement in Great Britain and Ireland

ISBN/EAN: 9783337298265

Printed in Europe, USA, Canada, Australia, Japan

Cover: Foto ©Thomas Meinert / pixelio.de

More available books at **www.hansebooks.com**

THE

EDINBURGH SYREN;

OR,

MUSICAL BOUQUET;

BEING A

NEW SELECTION OF MODERN SONGS,

SUNG AT THE

VARIOUS PLACES OF AMUSEMENT

IN

GREAT BRITAIN AND IRELAND.

EDINBURGH:

PRINTED FOR THOMAS BROWN, BOOKSELLER,
NO I. NORTH BRIDGE STREET.

MDCCXCII.

TO THE PUBLIC.

THE firſt impreſſion of this little volume having met with ſuch a favourable reception, has induced the Publiſher to iſſue another Edition, in which is inſerted a number of new Songs not to be had in any other ſmall Collection extant, and which, he hopes, will be found ſuited to every one's taſte, if we except thoſe that would in any degree tend to put the cheek of modeſty to the bluſh: And the Publiſher, conſcious of at leaſt endea-

vouring

vouring to " *Cull the Choiceſt*," now ſends it forth, with a view to promote the harmony and happineſs of thoſe who make Vocal Muſic a part of their Amuſement.

THE

Poor Jack.

GO patter to lubbers and fwabs d'ye fee,
 'Bout danger, and fear, and the like ;
A tight water boat, and good fea-room give me,
 And t'ent to a little I'll ftrike :
Tho' the tempeft top-gallant-mafts fmack fmooth
  fhould fmite,
 And fhiver each fplinter of wood,
Clear the wreck, ftow the yards, and boufe every
  thing tight,
 And under reef'd forefail we'll fcud :
Avaft, nor don't think me a milk-fop fo foft
 To be taken for trifles aback,
For they fay there's a Providence fits up aloft,
 To keep watch for the life of Poor Jack.

Why I heard the good chaplain palaver one day
 About fouls, heaven, mercy, and fuch,
And, my timbers, what lingo he'd coil and belay,
 Why 'twas juft all as one as high Dutch :

A 3

But he faid how a fparrow can't founder, d'ye fee,
   Without orders that comes down below,
And many fine things that prov'd clearly to me
   That Providence takes us in tow;
For fays he, do you mind me, let ftorms e'er fo oft
   Take the top fails of failors aback,
There's a fweet little cherub that fits up aloft,
   To keep watch for the life of Poor Jack.

I faid to our Poll, for you fee fhe would cry,
   When laft we weighed anchor for fea,
What argufies fniv'ling and piping your eye?
   Why what a damn'd fool you muft be:
Can't you fee the world's wide, and there's room
     for us all,
   Both for feamen and lubbers afhore;
And if to old Davy I fhould go friend Poll,
   Why you never will hear of me more:
What then, ail's a hazard, come don't be fo foft,
   Perhaps I may laughing come back,
For d'ye fee there's a cherub fits fmiling aloft,
   To keep watch for the life of Poor Jack.

D'ye mind me, a failor fhould be every inch
   All as one as a piece of a fhip,
And with her brave the world, without offering to
     flinch,
   From the moment the anchor's a trip:
As for me, in all weathers, all times, fides, and ends,
   Noughts a trouble from duty that fprings,
For my heart is my Poll's, and my rhino my friend's,
   And as for my life 'tis the king's:

Even when my time's come ne'er believe me fo foft
　As with grief to be taken aback,
That fame little cherub that fits up aloft,
　Will look out a good birth for Poor Jack.

The Tear that bedews Senfibility's Shrine.

Tho' Bacchus may boaft of his care killing bowl,
　And folly in thought drowning revels delight;
Such worfhip alas! hath no charms for the foul,
　When fofter devotions the fenfes invite:
　When fofter devotions the fenfes invite.

To the arrow of fate, or the canker of care,
　His potions oblivious a balm may beftow,
But to fancy that feeds on the charms of the fair,
　The death of reflection's the birth of all woe.
　The death, &c.

What foul that's poffeft of a dream fo divine,
　With riot would bid the fweet vifion begone,
For the tear that bedews fenfibility's fhrine,
　Is a drop of more worth than all Bacchus's tun.
　Is a drop, &c.

The tender excefs which enamours the heart,
　To few is imparted, to millions deny'd,

'Tis the brain of the victim that tempers the dart,
   And fools jeſt at that for which ſages have dy'd.
     And fools, &c.

Each change and exceſs hath thro' life been my
     doom,
   And well can I ſpeak of its joy and its ſtrife ;
The bottle affords us a glimpſe thro' the gloom,
   But love's the true ſunſhine that gladdens our
     life.
     But love's, &c.

Come then, roſy Venus, and ſpread oe'r my ſight,
   The magic illuſions that raviſh the ſoul,
Awake in my breaſt the ſoft dream of delight,
   And drop from thy myrtle one leaf in my bowl.
     And drop, &c.

Then deep will I drink of the nectar divine,
   Nor e'er jolly god from the banquet remove,
But each tube of my heart ever thirſt for the wine,
   That's mellow'd by friendſhip, and ſweeten'd
     by love.
     That's mellow'd, &c.

———————

The Maid that tends the Goats.

Up amang yon cliffy rocks,
Sweetly rings the riſing echo,
To the maid that tends the goats,
Lilting o'er her native notes.

Hark, fhe fings, " young Sandy's kind,
" An' he's promis'd ay to lo'e me,
" Here's a brotch I ne'er fhall tine,
" Till he's fairly marri'd to me;
" Drive away, ye drone time,
" An' bring about our bridal day.

" Sandy herds a flock o' fheep,
" Af'en does he blaw the whiftle,
" In a ftrain fae faftly fweet,   —
" Lam'mies lift'ning dare nae bleat;
" He's as fleet's the mountain roe,
" Hardy as the Highland heather,
" Wading thro' the winter fnow,
" Keeping ay his flock together:
" But a plaid, wi' bare houghs,
" He braves the bleakeft norlin blaft.

" Brawly he can dance and fing
" Canty glee, or Highland cronach;
" Nane can ever match his fling
" At a reel, or round a ring;
" Wightly can he wield a rung,
" In a brawl he's ay the bangfter,
" A' his praife can ne'er be fung
" By the langeft winded fangfter
" Sangs that fing o' Sandy,
" Come fhort, tho' they were e'er fae lang.

How Sweet the Love.

When firſt I ken'd young Sandy's face,
He ſung and look'd wi' ſic a grace,
    He ſung and look'd wi' ſic a grace,
He ſtole my heart but did na care,
The lad he loo'd a laſs more fair,
And oft I ſung o'er brae and burn
How ſweet the love that meets return.

He loo'd a laſs wi' fickle mind,
Was ſometimes cauld and ſometimes kind,
Which made the love ſick laddie rue,
For ſhe was cauld when he was true ;
He mourn'd and ſung o'er brae and burn,
How ſweet the love that meets return.

One day a pretty wreath he twin'd,
Where li'lacks with ſweet cowſlips join'd,
To make a garland for her hair,
But ſhe refus'd a gift ſo fair.
This ſcorn, he cry'd, can ne'er be borne,
But ſweet the love that meets return.

Juſt then he met my tell tale e'en,
And love ſo true is ſooneſt ſeen.
Dear laſs, ſaid he, my heart is thine,
For thy ſoft wiſhes are like mine,
Now Jenny in her turn may mourn,
How ſweet the love that meets return.

My anfwer was both frank and kind,
I loo'd the lad and tell'd my mind,
To kirk we went wi' hearty glee,
And wha fa bleft as he and me;
Now blithe we fing o'er brae and burn,
How fweet the love that meets return.

When the Fancy-ftirring Bowl.

WHEN the fancy-ftirring bowl
  Wakes its world of pleafure,
Glowing vifions gild my foul,
  And life's an endlefs treafure;
Mem'ry decks my wafted heart,
  Frefh with gay defires,
Rays divine my fenfes dart,
  And kindling hope infpires.
      Then who'd be grave,
      When wine can fave
    The heavieft foul from finking;
      And magic grapes,
      Give angel fhapes
    To ev'ry girl we're drinking.

Here fweet benignity and love
  Shed their influence round me,
Gather'd ills of life remove,
  And leave me as they found me.
Tho' my head may fwim, yet true
  Still to nature's feeling;

Peace and beauty fwim there too,
  And rock me as I'm reeling.
      Then who'd be grave, &c.

On youth's foft pillow tender truth
  Her penfive leffon taught me,
Age foon mock'd the dream of youth,
  And wifdom wak'd and caught me,
A bargain then with love I knock'd
  To hold the pleafing gipfey,
Then wife to keep my bofom lock'd,
  But turn the key when tipfey.
      Then who'd be grave, &c.

When time affuag'd my heated heart,
  The grey-beard blind and fimple,
Forgot to cool one little part
  Juft flufh'd by Lucy's dimple.
That part's enough of beauty's type
  To warm an honeft fellow;
And though it touch me not when ripe,
  It melts ftill while I'm mellow.
      Then who'd be grave, &c.

I'd rather be excus'd.

RETURNING from the fair one eve,
  Acrofs yon verdant plain,
Young Harry faid he'd fee me home;
  A tight, a comely fwain.   †

He begg'd I would a fairing take,
    And would not be refus'd;
Then afk'd a kifs, I blufh'd and cry'd,
    I'd rather be excus'd.

You're coy, faid he, my pretty maid,
    I mean no harm I fwear;
Long time I have in fecret figh'd
    For you, my charming fair:
But if my tendernefs offend,
    And if my love's refus'd,
I'll leave you—what, alone? cry'd I,
    I'd rather be excus'd.

He prefs'd my hand, and on we walk'd,
    He warmly urg'd his fuit;
But ftill to all he faid I was
    Moft obftinately mute.
At length, got home, he angry cry'd,
    My fondnefs is abus'd;
Then die a maid—indeed, faid I,
    I'd rather be excus'd.

The Jovial Tars.

COME, come, my jolly lads!
    The wind's abaft;
Brifk gales our fails fhall crowd.
Come buftle, buftle, boys,
    Haul the boat;
The boatfwain pipes aloud:

B

The ſhip's unmoor'd;
All hands on board;
The riſing gale
Fills every ſail,
The ſhip's well man'd and ſtor'd.
　Then ſling the flowing bowl—
　　Fond hopes ariſe—
　　The girls we prize
　Shall bleſs each jovial ſoul:
　　The can, boys bring—
　　We'll drink and ſing,
　While foaming billows roll.

Tho' to the Spaniſh coaſt
　We're bound to ſteer,
We'll ſtill our rights maintain;
Then bear a hand, be ſteady, boys,
　Soon we'll ſee
Old England once again:
　From ſhore to ſhore
　While cannons roar,
　Our tars ſhall ſhow
　The haughty foe,
Britannia rules the main.
　Then ſling the flowing bowl, &c.

Cobler of Caſtlebury.

'Twas in a village near Caſtlebury,
　A cobler and his wife did dwell,

And for a time no two fo merry,
   Their happinefs no tongue can tell;
But to this couple, the neighbours tell us,
   Something did happen that caus'd much ftrife,
For going to a neighb'ring alehoufe,
   The man got drunk and beat his wife.

But though he treated her fo vilely,
   What did this wife, good creature, do ?
Kept fnug, and found a method flily,
   To wring his heart quite through and through;
For Dick the tapfter, and his mafter,
   By the report that then was rife,
Were both in hopes by this difafter,
   To gain the cobler's pretty wife.

While things went on to rack and ruin,
   And all their furniture was fold,
She feem'd t' approve what each was doing,
   And got from each a purfe of gold.
So when the cobler's cares were over,
   He fwore to lead an alter'd life,
To mind his work, ne'er be a rover,
   And love no other but his wife.

The Lafs of Richmond Hill.

On Richmond Hill there lives a lafs,
   More bright than May-day morn ;
Whofe charms all other maids furpafs,
   A rofe without a thorn.

This lafs' fo neat, with fmiles fo fweet,
Has won my right good-will ;
I'd crowns refign to call her mine,
Sweet lafs of Richmond Hill.

Ye zephyrs gay that fan the air,
And wanton thro' the grove ;
O whifper to my charming fair—
I die for her and love.
This lafs fo neat, &c.

How happy will the fhepherd be,
Who calls this nymph his own ;
O may the choice be fix'd on me—
Mine's fix'd on her alone.
This lafs fo neat, &c.

Paddy Bull's Expedition.

WHEN I took my departure from Dublin's fweet
town,
And for England's ownfelf thro' the feas I did
plow ;
For four long days I was tofs'd up and down,
Like a quid of chew'd hay in the throat of a
cow ;
While afraid off the deck in the ocean to flip, Sir,
I clung like a cat a faft hold for to keep, Sir ;
Round about the big poft that grows out of the
fhip, Sir,
O I never thought more to fing langolee.

Thus ſtanding ſtock ſtill, all the while I was mov-
   ing,
  Till Ireland's coaſt I ſaw clean out of ſight ;
Myſelf the next day a true Iriſhman proving,
   When leaving the ſhip on the ſhore for to light;
As the board thcy put out was too narrow to
   quarter,
  The firſt ſtep I took was in ſuch a totter,
That I jump'd upon land, to my neck up in water;
    O that was no time to ſing langolee.

But as ſharp cold and hunger I never yet knew
   more,
  And my ſtomach and bowels did grumble and
   growl,
I thoughtthe beſtway to get each in good humour,
  Was to take out the wrinkles of both, by my
   ſoul ;
So I went to a houſe where roaſt meat they pro-
   vide, Sir,
  With a whirligig, whichup the chimney I ſpy'd,
   Sir,
And which grinds all their ſmoke into powder be-
   ſides, Sir—
    'Tis true as I am now ſinging langolee.

Then I went tothe landlordof allthe ſtage coaches,
  That ſet ſail for London each night of the week,
To whom I obnoxiouſly made my approaches,
  As a birth aboard one I was come for to ſeek;
But as for the inſide, I'd no caſh in my caſket,

Says I, with your leave, I make bold, Sir, to afk it,
When the coach is gone off, pray what time goes
 the bafket ?
  For there I can ride and fing langolee.

When, making his mouth up——" the bafket, fays
 he, Sir,
 Goes after the coach a full hour or two ;"
Very well, Sir, fays I, that's the thing then for
 me, Sir,
 But the Devil a word that he told me was true ;
For though one went before, and the other be-
 hind, Sir,
  They fat off cheek by jole at the very fame
  time, Sir,
So the fame day, at night, I fet out by moon-fhine,
 Sir,
  All alone by myfelf finging langolee.

O long life to the moon, for a brave noble crea-
 ture,
 That ferves us with lamp-light each night in
  the dark !
While the fun only fhines in the day, which, by
 nature,
 Wants no light at all——as you all may remark ;
But as for the moon, by my foul I'll be bound, Sir,
 It would fave the whole nation a great many
  pounds, Sir,
To fubfcribe for to light him up all the year round,
 Sir,
  Or I'll never fing more about langolee.

Anacreon.

To Anacreon in heav'n, where he fat in full glee,
  A few fons of harmony fent a petition,
That he their infpirer and patron would be ;
  When this anfwer arriv'd from the jolly old
    Grecian,
      Voice, fiddle and flute,
      No longer be mute,
I'll lend you my name and infpire you to boot ;
  And befides, I'll inftruct ye, like me, to en-
    twine,
  The myrtle of Venus with Bacchus's vine.

The news through Olympus immediately flew,
  When old Thunder pretended to give himfelf
    airs,
If thefe mortals are fuffer'd their fchemes to purfue,
  The devil a goddefs will ftay above ftairs.
      Hark ! already they cry,
      In tranfports of joy,
  Away to the fons of Anacreon we'll fly :
And there with good fellows, we'll learn to en-
    twine
The myrtle of Venus with Bacchus's vine.

The yellow hair'd god, and his nine fufty maids,
  From Helicon's banks will incontinent flee ;
Idalia will boaft but of tenantlefs fhades,
  And the beforked hill a mere defart will be :

My thunder, no fear on't,
Shall foon do it's errand,
And dam'me! I'll fwinge the ringleaders, I
warrant,
I'll trim the young dogs for thus daring to 'twine
The myrtle of Venus with Bacchus's vine.

Apollo rofe up, and faid prithee ne'er quarrel,
Good king of the gods, with my vot'ries below;
Your thunder is ufelefs, then fhowing his laurel,
Cry'd *Sic evitabile fulmen*, you know!
Then over each head
My laurels I'll fpread,
So my fons from your crackers no mifchief fhall
dread,
While fnug in their club-room, they jovially 'twine
The myrtle of Venus with Bacchus's vine.

Next Momus rofe up, with his rifible phiz,
And fwore with Apollo he'd cheerfully join:
The full tide of harmony ftill fhall be his,
But the fong and the catch, and the laugh fhall
be mine;
Then, Jove, be not jealous
Of thefe honeft fellows;
Cry'd Jove, we relent, fince the truth you now
tell us,
And fwear by old Styx, that they long fhall entwine
The myrtle of Venus with Bacchus's vine.

Ye fons of Anacreon, then join hand in hand,
Preferve unanimity, friendfhip, and love,

'Tis yours to fupport what's fo happily plann'd,
  You've the fanction of gods, and the fiat of Jove:
    While thus we agree,
    Our toaft let it be,
May our club flourifh happy, united and free !
And long may the fons of Anacreon entwine,
The myrtle of Venus with Bacchus's vine.

Bonny Bet.

No more I'll court the town bred fair,
  Who fhines in artificial beauty,
For native charms, without compare,
  Claim all my love, refpect, and duty.

CHORUS.

O my bonny, bonny Bet, fweet bloffom,
  Was I a king fo proud to wear thee,
From off the verdant couch I'd bear thee,
  To grace thy faithful lover's bofom.
    O my bonny, bonny Bet, &c.
Yet, afk me where thofe beauties lie,
  I cannot fay in fmile or dimple,
In blooming cheeks or radiant eye,
  'Tis happy nature wild and fimple.
    O my bonny, bonny Bet, &c.

Let dainty beaux for ladies pine,
  And figh in numbers trite and common,

Ye gods one darling wifh be mine,
And all I afk is lovely woman.
    O my bonny, bonny Bet, &c.

Come deareft girl, the rofy bowl,
    Like thy bright eye with pleafure dancing,
My heaven art thou, fo take my foul,
    With rapture every ferfe entrancing.
        O my bonny, bonny Bet, &c.

Golden Days of Good Queen Befs.

To my mufe give attention, and deem it not myf-
    tery,
If we jumble together mufic, poetry, and hiftory,
The times to difplay in the reign of Queen Befs,
    Sir,
Whofe name and whofe memory pofterity may
    blefs, Sir.

CHORUS.

O the golden days of good Queen Befs.
Merry be the memory of good Queen Befs.

Then we laugh at the bugbears of dons and armadas,
With their gunpowder puffs, and their bluftering
    bravadoes ;
For he knew how to manage both the mufket and
    the bow, Sir,
And cou'd bring down a Spaniard juft as eafy as a
    crow, Sir,
        O the golden days, &c.

Then our ftreets were unpav'd, and our houfes
 were thatch'd, Sir,
Our windows were lattic'd, our doors only latch'd,
 Sir,
Yet fo few were the folks that would plunder and
 rob, Sir,
That the hangman was ftarving for the want of a
 job, Sir,
   O the golden days, &c.

Then our ladies with large ruffs tied round about
 the neck faft,
Would gobble up a pound of beef fteakes for their
 breakfaft ;
While a clofe quilted coif their noddles juft did
 fit, Sir,
And they trufs'd up as tight as a rabbit for the
 fpit, Sir,
   O the golden days, &c.

Then jerkins, and doublets, and yellow worfted
 hofe, Sir ;
With a pair of huge whifkers, was the drefs of our
 beaus, Sir ;
Strong beer they preferr'd to claret or to hock
 Sir,
And no poultry they priz'd like the wing of an ox,
 Sir.
   O the golden days, &c.

Good neighbourhood was then as plenty too as
    beef, Sir,
And the poor from the rich ne'er wanted relief,
    Sir ;
While merry went the mill-clack, the ſhuttle and
    the plough, Sir,
And honeſt men could live by the ſweet of their
    brow, Sir,
        O the golden days, &c.

Then the folks every Sunday went twice at leaſt
    to the church, Sir,
And never left the parſon on the ſermon in the
    lurch, Sir ;
For they judg'd the Sabbath was for people to be
    good in,
And they thought it Sabbath-breaking if they
    din'd without pudding.
        O the golden days, &c.

Then our great men were good, and our good men
    were great, Sir,
And the props of the nation were the pillars of the
    ſtate, Sir ;
For the ſov'reign and the ſubjeɕt one intereſt ſup-
    ported,
And our powerful alliance by all powers then was
    courted.
        O the golden days, &c.

'Thus renown'd as they liv'd all the days of their
 lives, Sir,
Bright examples of glory to thofe who furvive, Sir;
May we their defcendants purfue the fame ways,
 Sir,
That King George, like Queen Befs, may have
 his golden days, Sir,

CHORUS. h

And may a longer reign of glory and
 fuccefs,
Make his name eclipfe the fame of good
 Queen Befs.

The Moment Aurora.

THE moment Aurora peep'd into my room,
I put on my clothes and I call'd to my groom ;
And, my head heavy ftill, from the fumes of laft
 night,
Took a bumper of brandy to fet all things right;
And now were well faddled Fleet, Dapple, and
 Grey,
Who feem'd longing to hear the glad found hark
 away.

Will Whiftle by this had uncoupl'd his hourds,
Whofe ecftacy nothing could keep within bounds;
Firft forward came Jowler, then Scentwell, then
 Snare,
Three better ftaunch harriers ne'er ftarted a hare

C

Then Sweetlips, then Driver, then Staunch, and
    then Tray,
All ready to open at hark, hark away.

'Twas now by the clock about five in the morn,
And we all gallop'd off to the found of the horn;
Jack Gater, Bill Babler, and Dick at the gun,
And by this time the merry Tom Fairplay made
    one,
Who, while we were jogging on blithefome and
    gay,
Sung a fong, and the chorus was—Hark, hark
    away.

And now Jemmy Lurcher had every bufh beat,
And no figns of madam, nor trace of her feet ;
Nay, we juft had begun our fad fortunes to curfe,
When all of a fudden out ftarts Mrs Pufs ;
Men, horfes, and dogs, all the glad-call obey,
And echo was heard to cry—hark, hark away.

The chace was a fine one, fhe took o'er the plain,
Which fhe doubled, and doubled, and doubled
    again ;
Till at laft fhe to cover return'd out out of breath,
Where I and Will Whiftle were in at the death ;
Then in triumph for you I the hare did difplay,
And cry'd to the horns, my boys, hark, hark
    away.

The Taxes.

Hard hard are the times, is the cry, 'tis no won-
 der;
For with taxes we are fo moft devilifh kept under;
What with taxes on this thing, and taxes on
 'tother,
It's ftrange how we live, and bring both ends to-
 gether.
   Derry down, down, down derry down.

From the crown of the head to the foles of the
 feet,
We are tax'd in all things fo wonderous complete,
Bedaubed with ftamps, as with biles was old Job,
We had need of his patience to bear with the load.
   Derry down, &c.

The hat that defends me from cold and from rain,
And the gloves that I wear for a purpofe the fame,
E'en the fhoes on my feet, which 'bove all I can't
 want,
The leather they're made of muft pay for the ftamp.
   Derry down, &c.

For the light from the heavens we're forced to pay,
Elfe from our apartments to fhut out the day,
Then grovel in darknefs like moles in the ground,
For unlefs we pay tax, there's no light to be
 found.
   Derry down, &c.

If we light up a candle, 'tis ftill all the fame.
F`r there Billy Pit he is with us again ;
Th`re is no efcaping his mercilefs paws,
For he ftops every gap by his new excife laws.
Derry down, &c.

If our lives we would fpend in a bachelor ftate,
We're taxed becaufe we're in want of a mate,
If our minds they fhould alter, and we take a
    fpoufe,
The king muft be pay'd before we pay our vows.
Derry down, &c.

When married, altho' perhaps little to fpare,
Yet one ftill wifhes children that little to heir ;
Should heaven be pleas'd with our wifh to com-
    ply,
And fpoufe be laid up in bed for to cry,
Derry down, &c.

Be't boy, or be't girl, to him 'tis the fame,
He muft have his quota e're it get a name ;
Altho' ne'er a groat over to make our friends
    happy,
'Tis all the fame thing to this hard taxing chappie.
Derry down, &c.

Next minifters ftipend, their cefs, and impoft,
Enough a poor foul to caufe flee from his poft ;

There is no denying the law it enforces,
For we're burden'd with taxes like Leith carters
 horfes.
      Derry down, &c.

There is no door left open through which we can
  go,
No crevice nor corner but what he doth know;
At the gates of grim death he has fet up his pole,
And there's none enters there, but their friends
 muft pay toll.
      Derry down, &c.

Thus, fingle or married, or dead or alive,
There's nothing can fave us from paying our tythe;
So 'tis needlefs to grumble, but patient fubmit,
For howe'er hard the times be, there's few wifh
 to flit.
    Derry down, down, down derry down.

The Waterman.

I was, d'ye fec, a waterman,
 As tight and fpruce as any,
  'Twixt Richmond town
  And Horfly down,
 I earn'd an honeft penny;
None could of fortune's favours brag
 More than could lucky I,
     C 3

My cot was fnug, well fill'd my cag,
　My grunter in the fty.
　　With wherry tight
　　And bofom light
I cheerfully did row,
　And, to complete this princely life,
　Sure never man had friend and wife
Like my Poll and my partner Joe.

I roll'd in joys like thefe awhile,
　Folks far and near carefs'd me,
　　Till, woe is me,
　　So lubberly
　The prefs-gang came and prefs'd me:
How could I all thefe pleafures leave?
　How with my wherry part?
1 never fo took on to grieve,
　It wrung my very heart.
　　But when on board
　　They gave the word
To foreign parts to go,
　I rued the moment I was born,
　That ever I fhould thus be torn
From my Poll and my partner Joe.

I did my duty manfully,
　While on the billows rolling,
　　And night and day
　　Could find my way
　Blindfold to the main-top bowling,
Thus all the dangers of the main,
　Quickfands, and gales of wind,

I brav'd, in hopes to taſte again
   The joys I left behind :
     In climes afar,
     The hotteſt war,
Pour'd broadfides on the foe,
   In hopes thefe perils to relate,
   As by my fide attentive fat,
My Poll and my partner Joe.

At laſt it pleas'd his Majeſty
   To give peace to the nation,
     And honeſt hearts,
     From foreign parts,
   Came home for confolation :
Like light'ning—for I felt new life,
   Now fafe from all alarms—
I rufh'd, and found my friend and wife—
   Lock'd in each other's arms !
     Yet fancy not
     I bore my lot
Tame, like a lubber :—No,
   For feeing I was finely trick'd,
   Plump to the devil I fairly kick'd
My Poll and my partner Joe.

Anna's Urn.

Encompass'd in an angel's frame,
An angel's virtues lay ;

Too foon did heav'n affert the claim,
And call'd its own away;
   And call'd its own away.

My Anna's worth, my Anna's charms,
Muft never more return,
Muft never more return,
What now fhall fill thofe widow'd arms,
Ah! me, Ah! me, Ah! me, my Anna's urn.

The Jolly Fifherman.

I am a jolly fifherman,
  I catch what I can get,
Still going on my better's plan
  All's fifh that comes to net:
Fifh, juft like men, I've often caught,
  Crabs, gudgeons, poor John, codfifh,
And many a time to market brought,
  A dev'lifh fight of odd fifh.
Thus all are fifhermen through life,
  With wary pains and labour,
This baits with gold, and that a wife,
  And all to catch his neighbour:
    Then praife the jolly fifherman,
     Who takes what he can get,
    Still going on his betters' plan,
    All's fifh that comes to net.

The pike, to catch the little fry,
   Extends his greedy jaw,
For all the world, as you and I,
   Have feen your man of law:
He who to lazinefs devotes
   His time is fure a numb fifh;
And members who give filent votes
   May fairly be called dumb fifh,
Falfe friends to eels we may compare,
   The roach refembles true ones;
Like gold-fifh we find old ones rare,
   Plenty as herrings new ones.
       Then praife, &c.

Like fifh then mortals are a trade,
   And trap'd, and fold, and bought,
The old wife and the tender maid,
   Are both with tickling caught;
Indeed the fair are caught, 'tis faid,
If you but throw the line in,
With maggots, flies, or fomething red,
   Or any thing that's fhining:
With fmall fifh you muft lie in wait
   For thofe of high condition,
But 'tis alone a golden bait
   Can catch a learn'd phyfician,
       Then praife, &c.

'Twas in the good Ship Rover.

'Twas in the good fhip rover
  I failed the world around,
And for three years and over,
  I ne'er touch'd Britifh ground;
At length in England landed,
  I left the roaring main,
Found all relations ftranded,
And went to fea again.

That time bound ftraight to Portugal,
  Right fore and aft we bore;
But, when we'd made Cape Ortugal,
  A gale blew off the fhore:
She lay, fo did it fhock her,
  A log upon the main;
Till, fav'd from Davy's locker,
  We put to fea again.

Next in a frigate failing,
  Upon a fqually night,
Thunder and light'ning hailing
  The horrors of the fight,
My precious limb was lopped off,
  I when they'd eas'd my pain,
Thank'd God I was not popped off,
  And went to fea again.

Yet ſtill am I enabled
　　To bring up in life's rear,
Although I'm quite diſabled,
　　And lie in Greenwich tier;
The king, God bleſs his royalty,
　　Who fav'd me from the main,
I'll praiſe with love and loyalty,
　　But ne'er to ſea again.

High-mettled Racer.

See the courſe throng'd with gazers, the ſports
　　are begun,
The confuſion but hear!—I'll be at you fir—done,
　　done;
Ten thouſand ſtrange murmurs reſound far and
　　near,
Lords, hawkers, and jockies aſſail the tir'd ear:
While, with neck like a rainbow, erecting his
　　creſt,
Pamper'd, prancing, and pleas'd, his head touch-
　　ing his breaſt,
Scarcely ſnuffing the air, he's ſo proud and elate,
The high-mettled racer firſt ſtarts for the plate.

Now reynard's turn'd out, and o'er hedge and
　　ditch ruſh
Hounds, horſes, and huntſmen, all hard at his
　　bruſh;

They run him at length, and they have him at
    bay,
And by fcent and by view, cheat a long tedious
    way :
While, alike born for fports of the field or the
    courfe,
Always fure to come through a ftaunch and fleet
    horfe ;
When fairly run down, the fox yields up his
    breath,
The high-mettled racer is in at the death.

Grown aged, ufed up, and turn'd out of the
    ftud,
Lame, fpavin'd, and wind-gall'd, but yet with
    fome blood ;
While knowing poftilions his pedigree trace,
Tell his dam won this fweepftakes, his fire gain'd
    that race ;
And what matches he won to the oftlers count
    o'er,
As they loiter their time at fome hedge ale-houfe
    door,
While the harnefs fore galls, and the fpurs his
    fides goad,
The high-mettled racer's a hack on the road.

Till at laft, having labour'd, drudg'd early and
    late,
Bow'd down by degrees, he bends on to his fate.

Blind, old, lean, and feeble, he tugs round a mill,
Or draws fand, till the fand of his hour-glafs
    ftands ftill :
And now, cold and lifelefs, expos'd to the view,
In the very fame cart which he yefterday drew,
While a pitying crowd his fad relicks furrounds,
The high mettled racer is fold for the hounds.

In my pleafant Native Plains.

In my pleafant native plains,
    Wing'd with blifs each moment flew,
Nature there infpir'd the ftrains,
    Simple as the joys I knew ;
Jocund morn and ev'ning gay,
    Claim'd the merry merry roundelay,
      Claim'd the merry merry roundelay,

Fields and flocks, and fragrant flow'rs,
    All that health and joy impart,
Call'd for artlefs mufic's pow'rs ;
    Faithful echoes to the heart.
Happy hours, for ever gay,
    Claim'd the merry roundelay.

But the breath of genial fpring,
    Wak'd the warblers of the grove ;
Who, fweet birds, that heard you fing,
    Would not join the fong of love ?
Your fweet notes, and chantings gay,
    Claim'd the merry roundelay.
          D   †

How bleſt the Maid.

How bleſt the maid whoſe boſom
  No headſtrong paſſion knows,
Her days in joy ſhe paſſes,
  Her nights in calm repoſe ;
Where e'er her fancy leads her,
  No pain, no fear invades her,
But pleaſure without meaſure,
  From ev'ry object flows.

No pain, no fear, where e'er ſhe goes,
  How bleſt the maid whoſe boſom
No headſtrong paſſion knows,
  Her days in joys ſhe paſſes,
Her nights in calm repoſe ;
  Where e'er her fancy leads,
No pains no fear invades,
  No fear invades, no fear invades.

—————

The Tobacco-Box.—A Duet.

Thomas.

Tho' the fate of battle on to-morrow wait,
Let's not loſe our prattle now my charming Kate,
Till the hour of glory love ſhould now take place,
Nor damp the joys before you with a future caſe.

Kate.

Oh my Thomas ſtill be conſtant, ſtill be true,
Be but to your Kate, as Kate is ſtill to you ;
Glory will attend you ſtill, will make us bleſt,
With my firmeſt love my dear you're ſtill poſſeſt.

Thomas.

No new beauties taſted, I'm their arts above,
Three campaigns are waited, but not ſo my love,
Anxious ſtill about thee, thou art all I prize,
Never Kate, without thee, will I bung theſe eyes.

Kate.

Conſtant to my Thomas I will ſtill remain,
Nor think I will leave thy ſide the whole cam-
     paign,
But I'll cheriſh thee and ſtrive to make thee bold,
May'ſt thou ſhare the vict'ry, may'ſt thou ſhare
     the gold.

Thomas.

If by ſome bold action I the halbert bear,
Think what ſatisfaction when my rank you ſhare,
Dreſt like any lady fair from top to toe,
Fine lac'd caps and ruffles then will be your due.

Kate.

If a ſerjeant's lady I ſhould chance to prove,
Linen ſhall be ready always for my love ;
Never more will Kate the Captain's laundreſs be,
I'm too pretty, Thomas love, for all but thee.

Thomas.

Here, Kate, take my 'bacco box, a foldier's all,
If by Frenchmen's blows your Tom is doom'd to
    fall,
When my life is ended, thou may'ft boaft and
    prove,
Thoud'ft my firft, my laft, my only pledge of love.

Kate.

Here take back thy 'bacco box, thou'rt all to me,
Nor think but I will be near thee love to fee,
In the hour of danger let me always fhare,
I'll be kept no ftranger to my foldier's fare.

Thomas.

Check that rifing figh, Kate, ftop that falling tear,
Come, my pretty comrade, entertain no fear;
But may heav'n befriend us; hark! the drums
    command,
Now I will attend you.   Love I kifs your hand.

Kate.

I can't ftop thefe tears, though crying I difdain,
But muft own 'tis trying hard the point to gain:
May good heav'ns defend thee, conqueft on thee
    wait;
One kifs more, and then I give thee up to fate.

Both repeat the laft ⎫ Conqueft on me wait,
verfe, only Thomas ⎬ And yield myfelf to fate.
fays   ⎭

Robin Adair.

You're welcome to Paxton, Robin Adair,
You're welcome to Paxton, Robin Adair,
  How does Jonny Mackril do,
  Aye and Luke Gard'ner too,
Why did they not come with you, Robin Adair?

Come and fit down by me, Robin Adair,
Come and fit down by me, Robin Adair,
  And welcome you fhall be,
  To every thing that you fee,
Why did they not come with you, Robin Adair?

I will drink wine with you, Robin Adair,
I will drink wine with you, Robin Adair,
  Rum punch, aye, or brandy too,
  By my foul I'll get drunk with you,
Why did they not come with you, Robin Adair?

Then let us drink about, Robin Adair,
Then let us drink about, Robin Adair,
  Till we've drank a hogfhead out,
  Then we'll be fow nae doubt,
Why did they not come with you, Robin Adair?

The Bonny Bold Soldier.

I've plenty of lovers that fue me in vain,
My heart is with Willy far over the plain,

D 3

For handfome and witty, and brave is the fwain,
The bonny bold foldier young Willy's for me ;
For handfome and witty and brave is the fwain,
The bonny bold foldier young Willy's for me.
In the trumpet's fhrill found my foldier delights,
For honour, his king, and his country he fights,
He figh------------------ts figh--------ts,
For honour, his king, and his country he fights,
For honour, his king, and his conntry he fights.

I fhare with his drefs in the heart of a beau,
The doctor my pulfe feels and ne'er takes a fee,
The one is pedantic, the other all fhow ;
The one is pedantic, &c.
The bonny bold foldier young Willy's for me,
The bonny bold foldier, &c.
 The trumpet's fhrill found, &c.

The lawyer fo crafty I fly from in fear,
The dangling poet I fhun when I fee,
Once more, O ye powers, reftore me my dear,
Once more, O ye powers, &c.
The bonny bold foldier young Willy's for me,
The bonny bold foldier, &c.
 The trumpet's fhrill found, &c.

The Neglected Tar.

I sing the Britifh feaman's praife,
 A theme renown'd in ftory,

It well deferves more polifh'd lays ;
  Oh ! 'tis your boaft and glory.
When mad-brain'd war fpreads death around,
  By them you are protected ;
But when in peace the nation's found,
  Thefe bulwarks are neglected.
    Then, O ! protect the hardy tar,
      Be mindful of his merit ;
    And when again your plung'd in war,
      He'll fhew his daring fpirit.

When thickeft darknefs covers all,
  Far on the tracklefs ocean ;
When lightnings dart, when thunders roll,
  And all is wild commotion :
When o'er the bark the white-topp'd waves,
  With boift'rous fweep are rolling,
Yet coolly ftill, the whole he braves,
  Untam'd amidft the howling.
    Then, oh ! protect, &c.

When deep immers'd in fulph'rous fmoke,
  He feels a glowing pleafure ;
He loads his gun, he cracks his joke,
  Elated beyong meafure.
Though fore and aft the blood-ftain'd deck
  Should lifelefs trunks appear ;
Or fhould the veffel float a wreck,
  The failor knows no fear.
    Then, oh ! protect, &c.

When long becalm'd, on fouthern brine,
  Where fcorching beams affail him;
When all the canvafs hangs fupine,
  And food and water fail him;
Then oft he dreams of Britain's fhore,
  Where plenty ftill is reigning;
They call the watch, his rapture's o'er,
  He fighs, but fcorns complaining.
     Then, oh! protect, &c.

Or burning on that noxious coaft,
  Where death fo oft befriends him;
Or pinch'd by hoary Greenland froft,
  True courage ftill attends him:
No clime can this eradicate,
  He glories in annoyance;
He fearlefs braves the ftorms of fate,
  And bids grim death defiance.
     Then, oh! protect, &c.

Why fhould the man who knows no fear,
  In peace be then neglected?
Behold him move along the pier,
  Pale, meagre, and dejected!
Behold him begging for employ!
  Behold him difregarded!
Then, view the anguifh in his eye,
  And fay, are tars rewarded?
     Then, oh! protect, &c.

To them your deareft rights you owe,
  In peace then would you ftarve them?

What fay ye Britain's fons!—Oh! no,
  Protect them, and preferve them.
Shield them from poverty, and pain,
  'Tis policy to do it;
Or, when grim war fhall come again,
  Oh, Britons, ye may rue it!
    Then, oh! protect, &c.

The Union of Bacchus and Venus.

I'M a vot'ry of Bacchus, his godfhip adore,
And love at his fhrine gay libations to pour,
And Venus, bleft Venus, my bofom infpires;
For fhe lights in our fouls the moft fecret of fires:
Yet to neither, I fwear fole allegiance to hold,
My bottle and lafs, I by turns muft enfold;
For the fweeteft of unions that mortals can prove,
Is of Bacchus, gay god, and the goddefs of love:
For the fweeteft of unions that mortals can prove,
Is of Bacchus, gay god, and the goddefs of love.

When fill'd to the fair, the brifk bumper I hold,
Can the mifer furvey with fuch pleafure his gold?
The ambrofia of gods no fuch relifh can boaft,
If good port, fill your glafs, and fair Kitty's the
    toaft;
And the charms of your girl more angelic will be,
If her fopha's encircled with wreaths from his tree,
For the fweeteft of unions that mortals can prove.
Is of Bacchus, gay god, and the goddefs of love.

All partial diſtinctions I hate from my ſoul,
O give me my fair one, and give me my bowl;
Bliſs, reflected from either, will ſend to my heart
Ten thouſand ſweet joys which they can't have
    apart;
Go try it, ye ſmiling and gay looking throng,
And your heart ſhall in uniſon beat to my ſong,
That the ſweeteſt of unions that mortals can prove,
Is of Bacchus, gay god, and the goddeſs of love.

Favourite Indian Death Song.

THE ſun ſets in night, and the ſtars ſhun the day,
But glory remains when their lights fade away;
Begin ye tormentors, your threats are in vain,
For the ſon of ALKNOMOOK ſhall never complain.

Remember the arrows he ſhot from his bow;
Remember your chiefs by his hatchet laid low:
Why ſo ſlow? do you wait 'till I ſhrink from my
    pain?
No—the ſon of ALKNOMOOK ſhall never com-
    plain.

Remember the wood—where in ambuſh we lay,
And the ſcalps which we bore from your nation
    away:
Now the flame riſes faſt! you exult in my pain;
But the ſon of ALKNOMOOK ſhall never complain.

I go to the land where my father is gone;
His ghoſt ſhall rejoice in the fame of his ſon:
Death comes like a friend,—he relieves me from
   pain;
And the ſon of ALKNOMOOK has ſcorn'd to com-
   plain.

Mary Scot.

HAPPY's the love that meets return,
When in ſoft flames ſouls equal burn;
But words are wanting to diſcover
The torments of a hopeleſs lover.
Ye regiſters of heav'n relate,
If looking o'er the rolls of fate
Did ye there ſee me mark'd to marrow,
Mary Scot the flow'r of Yarrow?

Ah, no! her form's too heav'nly fair—
Her love the gods above muſt ſhare,
While mortals with deſpair implore her,
And at a diſtance due, adore her—
O, lovely maid! my doubts beguile,
Revive and bleſs me with a ſmile;
Alas! if not, you ſoon debar a
Sighing ſwain the banks of Yarrow.

Be huſh, ye fears,—I'll not deſpair,
My Mary's tender as ſhe's fair;
Then I'll go tell her all my anguiſh,
She is too good to let me languiſh.

With fuccefs crown'd, I'll not envy
The folks who dwell above the fky;
When Mary Scot's become my marrow,
We'll make a paradife of Yarrow.

The Rofe Tree.

Pat.

A Rose-tree full in bearing,
   Had fweet flow'rs fair to fee,
One rofe, beyond comparing,
   For beauty attracted me.
Tho' eager once to win it,
   Lovely, blooming, frefh, and gay,
I find a canker in it,
   And now throw it far away.

Norah.

How fine this morning early,
   The fun fhining clear and bright;
So late I lov'd you dearly,
   Tho' loft now each fond delight.
The clouds feem big with fhow'rs,
   Sunny beams no more are feen,—
Farewell ye happy hours,
   Your falfehood has chang'd the fcene.

Both repeat.

The clouds feem big, &c. to the end.

Dear is my native Vale.

Dear is my little native vale,
  The ring-dove builds and warbles there;
Clofe by my cot fhe tells her tale
  To ev'ry paffing villager.
The fquirrel leaps from tree to tree,
And fhells his nuts at liberty.

In orange groves and myrtle bow'rs,
  That breathe a gale of fragrance round,
I charm the fairy-footed hours,
  With my lov'd lute's romantic found;
Or crowns of living laurel weave
For thofe that win the race at eve.

The fhepherd's horn at break of day,
  The ballet danc'd in twilight glade,
The canzonet and roundelay,
  Sung in the filent greenwood fhade.
Thefe fimple joys, that never fail,
Shall bind me to my native vale.

For tendernefs fafhion'd.

For tendernefs fafhion'd, in life's early day,
A parent's foft forrow to mine led the way;
The leffon of pity was caught from her eye,
And ere I knew language, I fpoke with a figh.

E

The nightingale plunder'd,—the mate-widow'd
    dove,
The warbled complaint of the fuffering grove;
To youth as it ripen'd, gave fentiment new:
The object ftill changing, the fympathy true.

Soft embers of paffion yet reft in their glow;
A warmth of more pain may this breaft never
    know !
Or if too indulgent the bleffing I claim,
Let the fpark drop from reafon, that weakens the
    flame.

Mary's Dream.

THE moon had climb'd the higheft hill
    That rifes o'er the fource of Dee,
And from the eaftern fummit fhed
    Her filver light on tow'r and tree;
When Mary laid her down to fleep,
    Her thoughts on Sandy far at fea :
Then foft and low a voice was heard
    Say—Mary weep no more for me.

She from her pillow gently rais'd
    Her head, to afk who there might be,
And faw young Sandy fhivering ftand,
    With palid cheek and hollow eye.
O, Mary dear ! cold is my clay,
    It lies beneath a ftormy fea;

Far, far from thee, I ſleep in death,
   So Mary weep no more for me.

Three ſtormy nights and ſtormy days,
   We toſs'd upon the raging main,
And long we ſtrove our bark to ſave,
   But all our ſtriving was in vain :
Ev'n then when horror chill'd my blood,
   My heart was fill'd with love for thee.
The ſtorm is paſt, and I at reſt,
   So Mary weep no more for me.

O ! maiden dear ! thyſelf prepare,
   We ſoon ſhall meet upon that ſhore
Where love is free from doubt or care,
   And thou and I ſhall part no more.
Loud crow'd the cock ! the ſhadow fled !
   No more of Sandy could ſhe ſee ;
But ſoft the paſſing ſpirit ſaid,
   O ! Mary ! weep no more for me.

SONG. *Poor Soldier.*

Norah.

THE meadows look charming, the birds ſweetly
   ſing,
So gaily they carol the praiſes of ſpring ;
Tho' nature rejoices, poor Norah ſhall mourn,
Until her dear Patrick again ſhall return.

Ye laffes of Dublin, ah! hide your gay charms,
Nor lure my dear Patrick from Norah's fond arms
Tho' fattins, and ribbons, and laces are fine,
They hide not a heart with fuch feelings as mine.

The Bud of the Rofe.

Belville.

HER mouth, which a fmile,
Devoid of all guile,
   Half opens to view,
Is the bud of the rofe
In the morning that blows, .
   Impearl'd with the dew.

More fragrant her breath
Than the flow'r fcented heath
   At the dawning of the day,
The hawthorn in bloom,
'The lilly's perfume,
   Or the bloffoms of May.

The Tartan Plaid.

BY moonlight on the green,
   Where lads and laffes ftray,
How fweet the bloffom'd bean,
   How fweet the new-made hay ?

But not to me fae fweet
 The bloffom of the thorn,
As when my lad I meet
 More frefh than May-day morn.
  Give me the lad fo blithe and gay,
  Give me the tartan plaiddie ;
  For fpite of all the world can fay,
  I'll wed my Highland laddie.
His fkin is white as fnow,
 His een are bonny blue ;
Like rofe-bud fweet his mou
 When wet with morning dew.
Young Will is rich and great,
 And fain wou'd ca' me his ;
But what is pride or ftate
 Without love's fmiling blifs.
  Give me the lad, &c.
When firft he talk'd of love,
 He look'd fo blithe and gay,
His flame I did approve,
 And could nae fay him nay.
Then to the kirk I'll hafte,
 There prove my love aud truth;
Reward a love fo chafte,
 And wed the conftant youth.
  Give me the lad, &c.

The wealthy Fool.

THE wealthy fool with gold in ftore,
 Will ftill defire to grow richer;

Give me but thefe, I afk no more,
　My charming girl, my friend, and pitcher.

My friend fo rare, my girl fo fair,
　With thefe what mortal can be richer?
Give me but thefe, a fig for care,
　With my fweet girl, my friend, and pitcher.

From morning fun I'd never grieve
　To toil a hedger or a ditcher,
If that when I come home at eve
　I might enjoy my friend and pitcher.
　　My friend fo rare, &c.

Tho' fortune ever fhuns my door,
　I know not what 'tis can bewitch her;
With all my heart can I be poor—
　With my fweet girl, my friend, and pitcher.
　　My friend fo rare, &c.

Let Care be a Stranger.

LET care be a ftranger to each jovial foul
Who, Ariftippus like, can his paffions controul:
Of wifeft philofophers wifeft was he,
Who, attentive to eafe, let his mind ftill be free:
The Prince, Peer, or Peafant to him were the fame,
For pleas'd, he was pleafing to all where he came,
But ftill turn'd his back on contention and ftrife,
Refolving to live all the days of his life.

A friend to mankind, all mankind was his friend,
And the peace of his mind was his ultimate end ;
He found fault with none if none found fault with
   him,
If his friend had a humour, he humour'd his whim;
If wine was the word, why he bumper'd his glafs,
If love was the topic, he toafted his lafs ;
But ftill turn'd his back on contention and ftrife,
Refolving to live all the days of his life.

If councils difputed, if councils agreed,
He found fault with neither; for this was his creed,
That let them be guided by folly or fenfe,
'Twould be *femper eadem* an hundred years hence.
He thought 'twas unfocial to be mal-content,
If the tide went with him, with the tide too he went;
But ftill turn'd his back on contention and ftrife,
Refolving to live all the days of his life.

Was the nation at war, he wifh'd well to the fword;
If a peace was concluded, a peace was his word,
Difquiet to him, of body or mind,
Was the longitude only he never could find.
The philofopher's ftone was but gravel and pain,
And all who had fought it, had fought it in vain ;
He ftill turn'd his back on contention and ftrife,
Refolving to live all the days of his life.

Then let us all follow Ariftippus's rules,
And deem his opponents both affes and mules ;
Let thofe not contented to lead or to drive,
By the bees of their fex be drove out of the hive :

Expell'd from the manfions of quiet and eafe,
May they never find out the bleft art how to pleafe;
While our friends and ourfelves, not forgetting
    our wives,
By thofe maxims may live all the days of our
    our lives.

The gaily circling Glafs.

By the gaily circling glafs
We can fee how minutes pafs,—
By the hollow flafk are told
How the waining night grows old.

Soon, too foon, the bufy day
Drives us from our fports away:
What have we with day to do?
Sons of care—'twas made for you.

Come then fill the cheerful glafs,
Truth is only found in wine:
Tales of love are all a farce,
But true friendfhip is divine.

With a cheerful old Friend.

WITH a cheerful old friend, and a merry old fong,
And a tankard of porter, I'd fit the night long,

And laugh at the follies of thofe that repine,—
Tho' I muſt drink porter while they can drink
   wine.

I envy no mortal, be he ever fo great,—
Nor fcorn I the wretch for his lowly eſtate ;
But, what I abhor, and deem as a curfe,
Is meannefs of fpirit,—not poornefs of purfe.

Then let us, companions, be jovial and gay,
And cheerfully fpend live's remainder away ;
Upheld by a friend, our foes we'll defpife,—
For, the more we are envy'd, the higher we rife.

Brown Ale.

WHEN the chill Sirocco blows,
   And winter tells a heavy tale ;
When 'pyes and daws, and rooks and crows,
   Do fit and curfe the froft and fnows.
     Then give me ale !
Stout brown ale, nut-brown ale,—
     O give me nut-brown ale.

Ale in a Saxon rumkin then,
   Such as will make Grimalkin prate,
Bids valour burgeon in tall men ;
   Quickens the poet's wit and pen ;
     Defpifes fate—
Old brown ale, nut-brown ale,
     O give me ftout brown ale.

Ale that the plowman's heart up keeps,
   And equals it to tyrants thrones,
That wipes the eye which over weeps,
   And lulls in fweet and dainty fleeps
     The wearied bones.
Old brown ale, nut-brown ale——
     O give me ftout brown ale.

Wit, Women, and Wine.

WHEN Jove was refolv'd to create the round earth,
   He fubpœned the virtues divine,——
Young Bacchus he fat precedentum of mirth,
   And the toaft was " wit, women, and wine."

The fentiment tickl'd the ear of each god,——
   Apollo he wink'd at the nine ;
And Venus gave Mars, too, a fly wanton nod,
   When fhe drank to wit, women, and wine.

Old Jove fhook his fides, and the cup put around,
   While Juno, for once, look'd divine;
Thefe bleffings, fays he, fhall on earth now abound,
   And the toaft is wit, women, and wine.

Thefe are joys, worthy gods, which to mortals
     are given,
Says Momus, who will not repine ?
For what's worth our notice, pray tell me, in
     heav'n,
If man have wit, women, and wine?

This joke you'll repent, I'll lay fifty to feven,
    Such attraction no pow'r can decline ;
Old Jove, by yourfelf you will keep houfe in heav'n,
    For we'll follow wit, women, and wine.

Thou'rt right, fays old Jove, let us hence to the
    earth,
    Men and gods think variety fine ;
Who'd ftay in the clouds, when good nature and
    mirth
Are below with wit, women, and wine.

Rule Britannia.

WHEN Britain firft, at Heav'n's command,
    Arofe from out the azure main,
    Arofe, &c.
This was the charter, the charter of the land,
    And guardian angels fung the ftrain;

CHORUS.

    Rule Britannia, Britannia rule the waves,
    For Britons never will be flaves.

The nations not fo bleft as thee,
    Muft in their turns to tyrants fall,
    Muft, &c.
Whilft thou fhalt flourifh, fhalt flourifh great and
    free,
    The dread and envy of them all.
        Rule Britannia, &c.

Still more majeſtic ſhalt thou riſe—
  More dreadful from each foreign ſtroke,
  More dreadful, &c.
As the loud blaſt that tears the ſkies,
  Serves but to root thy native oak.
    Rule Britannia, &c.

Thee haughty tyrants ne'er ſhall tame ;
  All their attempts to bend thee down,
  All their, &c.
Will but arouſe, arouſe thy gen'rous flame,
  And work their woe and thy renown.
    Rule Britannia, &c.

To thee belongs the rural reign,—
  Thy cities ſhall with commerce ſhine,
  Thy cities, &c.
All thine ſhall be, ſhall be the ſubjeƈt main,
  And ev'ry ſhore its circles thine.
    Rule Britannia, &c.

The Muſes, ſtill with freedom found,
  Shall to thy happy coaſt repair,
  Shall to, &c.
Bleſs'd iſle ! with beauty, with matchleſs beauty
    crown'd,
    And manly hearts to guard the fair.

CHORUS.

Rule Britannia, Britannia rule the waves,
For Britons never will be ſlaves.

Neptune.

Had Neptune when firſt he took charge of the ſea,
Been as wiſe, or at leaſt been as merry as we,
He'd have thought better on't, and inſtead of the
　　brine,
Would have fill'd the vaſt ocean with generous
　　wine.

What trafficking then would have been on the main,
For the ſake of good liquor, as well as for gain!
No fear then of tempeſt, or danger of ſinking,—
The fiſhes ne'er drown that are always a drinking.

The hot thirſty ſun would then drive with more
　　haſte,
Secure in the evening of ſuch a repaſt;
And when he'd got tipſey, would have taken his
　　nap
With double pleaſure on Thetis's lap.

By the force of his rays, and thus heated with
　　wine,
Conſider how glorioully Phœbus would ſhine;
What vaſt exhalations he'd draw up on high
To relieve the poor earth as it wanted ſupply.

How happy us mortals, when bleſt with ſuch rain,
To fill all our veſſels, and fill them again!
Nay, even the beggar, that has ne'er a diſh,
Might jump in the river and drink like a fiſh.
F

What mirth and contentment in every one's brow—
Hob, as great as a prince, dancing after his plow!
The birds in the air, as they play on the wing,
Altho' they but fip, would eternally fing.

The ftars, which, I think, don't to drinking in-
    cline,
Would frifk and rejoice at the fume of the wine;
And, merrily twinking, would foon let us know,
That they were as happy as mortals below.

Had this been the cafe, what had we then enjoy'd?
Our fpirits ftill rifing, our fancy ne'er cloy'd!
A pox then on Neptune, when 'twas in his pow'r,
To flip, like a fool, fuch a fortunate hour.

The Tinker.

A TINKER I am, my name's Natty Sam,
    From morn to night I trudge it;
So low is my fate, my pers'nal eftate
    Lies all within my budget.

CHORUS.

Work for the tinker, ho! good wives,
    For they are lads of mettle;
'Twere well if you could mend your lives
    As I can mend a kettle.

The man of war, the man of the bar,
    Phyſicians, prieſts, free-thinkers,
That rove up and down great London town,
    What are they all? but tinkers.
      Work for the tinker, &c.

Thoſe among the great, who tinker the ſtate,
    And badger the minority;
Pray what's the end of their work, my friend?
    But to rivet a good majority.
      Work for the tinker, &c.

This mends his name, that cobles his fame,
    that tinkers his reputation;
And thus, had I time, I could prove in my rhime,
    Jolly tinkers of all the nation.
      Work for the tinker, &c.

A Soldier's Life.

THIS, this my lad's a ſoldier's life;
He marches to the ſprightly fife,
And in each town to ſome new wife
    Swears he'll be ever true.
He's here, he's there, where is he not?
Variety's his envy'd lot;
He eats, drinks, ſleeps, and pays no ſhot,
    And follows the loud tattoo.

Call'd out to face his country's foes,
The tears of fond, domeſtic woes,
He kiſſes off, and boldly goes
   To earn of fame his due.
Religion, liberty, and laws,
Both his are, and his country's cauſe,
For theſe thro' danger, without pauſe,
   He follows the loud tattoo.

And if at laſt in honour's wars,
He earns his ſhare of danger's ſcars,——
Still he feels bold, and thanks his ſtars
   He's no worſe fate to rue.
At Chelſea, free from toil and pain,
He wields his crutch, points out the ſlain,
And, in fond fancy, once again
   Follows the loud tattoo.

━━━━━━━━

Nothing like Grog.

A ᴘʟᴀɢᴜᴇ of theſe muſty old lubbers,
 Who tell us to faſt and to think,
And patient fall in with life's rubbers,
 With nothing but water to drink.
A can of good ſtuff, had they twigg'd it,
 Would have ſet them for pleaſure agog,
  And in ſpite of the rules,
  The rules of the ſchools,
The old fools would have all of them ſwigg'd it,
 And ſwore there was nothing like grog.

My father, when laſt I from Guinea
  Return'd with abundance of wealth,
Cry'd Jack, never be ſuch a ninny
  To drink ;—ſays I,—father, your health !
So I paſt round the ſtuff, and he twigg'd it,
  And it ſet the old codger agog ;
      And he ſwigg'd, and mother,
      And ſiſter, and brother,
And I ſwigg'd, and all of us ſwigg'd it,
  And ſwore there was nothing like grog.

One day when the chaplain was preaching,
  Behind him I curiouſly ſlunk,
And, while he our duty was teaching,
  As how we ſhould never get drunk,
I tipt him the ſtuff, and he twigg'd it,
  Which ſoon ſet his rev'rence agog;
      And he ſwigg'd, and Nick ſwigg'd,
      And Ben ſwigg'd, and Dick ſwigg'd,
And I ſwigg'd, and all of us ſwigg'd it,
  And ſwore there was nothing like grog.

Then truſt me, there's nothing as drinking
  So pleaſant on this ſide the grave,
It keeps the unhappy from thinking,
  And makes 'em more valiant, more brave ;
For me from the moment I twigg'd it,
  The good ſtuff has ſo ſet me agog,
      Sick or well, late or early,
      Wind foully or fairly,
I've conſtantly, conſtantly ſwigg'd it ;
  And d—mne me, there's nothing like grog.

Jack Ratlin.

JACK RATLIN was the ableft feaman,
  None like him could hand, reef, or fteer ;
No dang'rous toil, but he'd encounter
  With fkill, and in contempt of fear.
In fight a lion,—the battle ended,
  Meek as the bleating lamb he'd prove ;
Thus Jack had manners, courage, merit,
  Yet did he figh,—and all for love.

The fong the jeft, the flowing liquor,
  For none of thefe had Jack's regard ;
He, while his meffmates were curoufing,
  High fitting on his pending yard,
Would think upon his fair one's beauties,
  Swear never from fuch charms to rove ;
That truly he'd adore them living,
  And, dying, figh—to end his love.

The fame exprefs the crew commanded
  Once more to view their native land,
Amongft the reft brought Jack fome tidings ;
  Would it had been his love's fair hand !
Oh ! Fate ! her death defac'd the letter—
  Inftant his pulfe forgot to move !
With quiv'ring lips, and eyes uplifted,
  He heav'd a figh !—and dy'd for love.

The Sailor's Song.

When it is night, and the mid-watch is come,
  And chilling mifts hang o'er the darken'd main,
Then failors think of their far diftant home,
  And of thofe friends they ne'er may fee again.
      But when the fight's begun,
      Each ferving at his gun,
Should any thought of them come o'er your mind,—
    Think, only, fhould the day be won,
      How 'twill cheer
      The heart, to hear
    That their old companion—he was one.

Or, my lad, if you a miftrefs kind
  Have left on fhore,—fome pretty girl and true,
Who many a night doth liften to the wind,
  And figh to think how it may fare with you ;
      O ! when the fight's begun,
      And ferving at his gun,
Should any thought of her come o'er your mind—
    Think, only fhould the day be won,
      How 'twill cheer
      Her heart, to hear
    That her own true failor—he was one.

Sweet Poll of Plymouth.

Sweet Poll of Plymouth was my dear,
  When forc'd from her to go ;—

Adown her cheeks rain'd many a tear,
 My heart was fraught with woe.—
Our anchor weigh'd, for fea we ftood,
 The land we left behind ;
Her tears then fwell'd the briny flood,
 My fighs increas'd the wind.

We plow'd the deep, and now between
 Us lay the ocean wide ;
For five long years I had not feen
 My fweet, my bonny bride.
That time I fail'd the world around,
 All for my true love's fake ;
But prefs'd as we were homeward bound,
 I thought my heart would break.

The prefs-gang bold I afk'd in vain
 To let me once on fhore ;
I long'd to fee my Poll again,
 But faw my Poll no more.
And have they torn my love away !
 And is he gone !—fhe cry'd ;
My Polly—fweeteft flow'r of May,
 She languifh'd, droop'd, and dy'd.

Death or Liberty.

Whilst happy in my native land,
 I boaft my country's charter ;
I'll never bafely lend my hand
 Her liberties to barter.

The noble mind is not at all
   By poverty degraded;
'Tis guilt alone can make us fall,
   And well I am perfuaded,
Each freeborn Briton's fong fhall be,
   Give me death or liberty.
      Give me death, &c.

Tho' fmall the pow'r which fortune grants,
   And few the gifts fhe fends us,
The lordly hireling often wants
   That freedom which defends us:
By law fecur'd from lawlefs ftrife,
   Our houfe is our caftellum;
Thus blefs'd with all that's dear in life,
   For lucre fhall we fell 'em?
No!—ev'ry Briton's fong fhall be,
Give me death or liberty.
      Give me death, &c.

The Sailor's Farewell.

THE top-fail fhivers in the wind,
   The fhip fhe cafts to fea,
But yet, my foul, my heart, my mind,
   Are, Mary, moor'd with thee;
For tho' thy failor's bound afar,
Still love fhall be his leading ftar.

Should landſmen flatter when we're fail'd,
   O doubt their artful tales ;
No gallant failor ever fail'd,
   If iove breath'd conſtant gales ;
Thou art the compaſs of my ſoul,
Which ſteers my heart from pole to pole.

Syrens in every port we meet,
   More fell than rocks and waves ;
But ſuch as grace the Britiſh fleet,
   Are lovers, and not ſlaves ;
No foes our courage ſhall ſubdue,
Altho' we've left our hearts with you.

Theſe are our cares—but if you're kind,
   We'll fcorn the daſhing main,
The rocks, the billows, and the wind,
   The power of France and Spain :
Now England's glory reſts with you,
Our ſails are full—ſweet girls adieu !

A little Love, but urg'd with Care.

Somehow my ſpindle I miſlaid,
   And loft it underneath the graſs ;
Damon advancing, bow'd his head,
   And ſaid, what feek you pretty laſs ?
     A little love, but urg'd with care.
     Oft leads a heart, and leads it far.

'Twas paffing by yon fpreading oak,
   That I my fplindle loft juft now:
His knife then kindly Damon took,
   And from the tree he cut a bough.
     A little love, &c.

Thus did the youth his time employ,
   While me he tenderly beheld;
He talk'd of love, I leap'd for joy,
   For ah! my heart did fondly yield.
     A little love, &c.

Ma chere Amie.

Ma chere amie, my charming fair,
Whofe fmiles can banifh ev'ry care;
In kind compaffion fmile on me,
Whofe only care is love of thee.
   Ma chere amie, ma chere amie, ma chere amie,
     ma chere amie.

Under fweet friendfhip's facred name,
My bofom caught the tender flame;
May friendfhip in thy bofom be
Converted into love for me.
     Ma chere amie, &c.

Together rear'd, together grown,
O let us now unite in one!

Let pity foften thy decree,
I droop, dear maid·! I die for thee.
    Ma chere amie, &c.

The Rofe.

No flower that blows is like this rofe,
    Or fcatters fuch perfume ;
Upon my breaft, ah! gently reft,
    And ever, ever bloom !

Dear pledge to prove a parent's love,
    A pleafing gift thou art ;
Come, fweeteft flower, and from this hour
    Live henceforth in my heart !

Rofina.

Ere bright Rofina met my eyes,
    How peaceful paft the joyous day !
In rural fports 1 gain'd the prize,
    Each virgin liften'd to my lay.

But now no more I touch the lyre,
    No more the ruftic fports can pleafe ;
I live the flave of fond defire,
    Loft to myfelf, to mirth, and eafe.

The tree that, in a happier hour,
   Its boughs extended o'er the plain,
When blaſted by the lightning's pow'r,
   Nor charms the eye, nor ſhades the ſwain.

The honeſt Sailor.

THAT girl who fain wou'd chuſe a mate,
   Shou'd ne'er in fondneſs fail her ;
May thank her lucky ſtars, if Fate
   Should ſplice her to a ſailor.

He braves the ſtorm, the battle's heat,
   The yellow boys to nail her ;
Diamonds, if diamonds ſhe could eat,
   Wou'd ſeek her honeſt ſailor.

If ſhe be true, ſure of his heart,
   She never need bewail her ;
For tho' a thouſand leagues apart,
   Still conſtant is her ſailor.

Tho' ſhe be falſe, ſtill he is kind,
   And comes with ſmiles to hail her ;
He truſting, as he truſts the wind,
   Still faithleſs to her ſailor.

A butcher can procure her prog ;
   three threads to drink, a taylor :

G

What's that to bifcuit and to grog
    Procur'd her by her failor ?

She who wou'd fuch a mate refufe,
    The devil fure muft ail her :
Search round, and if you're wife, you'll chufe
    To wed an honeft failor.

Love in low Life.

Young Jockey he courted fweet Moggy fo fair,
The lafs fhe was lovely, the fwain debonair :
They hugg'd, and they cuddl'd, and talk'd with
        their eyes,
And look'd, as all lovers do, wonderful wife.

A fortnight was fpent, ere dear Moggy came too;
(For maidens a decency keep when they woo);
At length fhe confented, and made him a vow :
And Jockey he gave for her jointure his cow.

They pannel'd their dobbins, and rode to the fair;
Still kiffing and fondling until they came there,
They call'd on the parfon, and by him were wed,
And Moggy fhe took her dear Jockey to bed.

They ftaid there a week, as the neighbours all fay,
And none were fo happy and gamefome as they :
Then home they return'd, but return'd moft un-
        kind,
For Jockey rode on, and left Moggy behind.

Surpris'd at this treatment, fhe cry'd Gaffer Jock,
Pray what is the reafon that Moggy you mock?
Quoth he, Goofe, come on, why you're now my
    bride;
And when volk are wed, they fet fooling afide.

He took home his Moggy, good conduct to learn,
Who brufh'd up the houfe while he thatch'd the
    old barn;
They laid in a ftock for the cares that enfue,
And now live as man and wife ufually do.

On Friendfhip.

THE world, my dear Myra, is full of deceit,
And friendfhip's a jewel we feldom can meet;
How ftrange does it feem, that in fearching around,
This fource of content is fo rare to be found.

O friendfhip! thou balm and rich fweetner of life,
Kind parent of eafe, and compofer of ftrife;
Without thee, alas! what are riches and pow'r,
But empty delufion, the joys of an hour?

How much to be priz'd and efteem'd is a friend,
On whom we may always with fafety depend;
Our joys when extended, will always increafe,
And griefs, when divided, are hufh'd into peace.

G 2

When fortune is fmiling, what crowds will ap-
    pear,
Their kindnefs to offer, and friendfhip fincere ;
Yet change but the profpect, and point out dif-
    trefs,
No longer to court you they eagerly prefs.

Heigho! that I for Hunger fhould die !

A voyage over feas had not enter'd my head,
Had I known on which fide to have butter'd my
    bread.
      Heigho ! fure I—for hunger muft die !
I've fail'd like a booby ; come here in a fquall,
Where alas! there's no bread to be butter'd at all!
      Oho ! I'm a terrible booby !
      Oh, what a loft mutton am I !

In London, what gay chop-houfe figns in the ftreet!
But only the fign here is of nothing to eat.
      Heigho ! that I for hunger fhou'd die !
My mutton's all loft, I'm a poor ftarving elf.
And all for the world like a loft mutton myfelf.
      Oho ! I fhall die a loft mutton !
      Oh, what a loft mutton am I !

For a neat flice of beef, I cou'd roar like a bull,
And my ftomach's fo empty, my heart is quite full.
      Heigho ! that I—for hunger fhou'd die !

But grave without meat, I muſt here meet my
    grave,
For my bacon, I fancy, I never ſhall ſave.
       Oho ! I ſhall ne'er ſave my bacon !
       I can't ſave my bacon, not I !

———

Duet. *Inkle and Yarico.*

Inkle.

O say, ſimple maid, have you form'd any notion
Of all the rude dangers in croſſing the ocean ?
When winds whiſtle ſhrilly, ah ! won't they re-
    mind you
To ſigh with regret for the grot left behind you?

Yarico.

Ah ! no, I could follow, and ſail the world over,
Nor think of my grot, when I look at my lover !
The winds which blow round us, your arms for
    my pillow,
Will lull us to ſleep, whilſt we're rock'd by each
    billow.

Inkle.

" Then ſay, lovely laſs, what if haply eſpying
A rich gallant veſſel with gay colours flying?

G 3

Yarico.

I'll journey with thee, love, to where the land
   narrows.
And fling all my cares at my back with my arrows."

Both.

O fay then, my true love, we never will funder,
Nor fhrink from the tempeft, nor dread the big
   thunder ;
Whilft conftant, we'll laugh at all changes of
   weather,
And journey all over the world both together.

The general Toaſt.

HERE's to the maiden of bafhful fifteen,
   Likewife to the widow of fifty ;
Here's to the bold and extravagant quean,
   And here's to the houfewife that's thrifty,
      Let the toaft pafs,
      Drink to the lafs,
I'll warrant fhe'll prove an excufe for the glafs,

Here's to the maiden whofe dimples we prize,
   And likewife to her that has none, Sir,
Here's to the maid with a pair of blue eyes,
   And here's to her that's but one, Sir.
      Let the toaft pafs, &c.

Here's to the maid with a bosom of snow,
 And to her that's as brown as a berry ;
And here's to the wife with a face full of woe,
 And here's to the girl that's merry.
   Let the toast pass, &c.

Let her be clumsy, or let her be slim,
 Young or ancient I care not a feather,
So fill the pint bumper quite up to the brim,
 And e'en let us toast them together.
   Let the toast pass,
   Drink to the lass,
I'll warrant she'll prove an excuse for the glass.

The Blush of Aurora.

The blush of Aurora now tinges the morn,
And dew-drops bespangle the sweet-scented thorn ;
Then, sound, brother sportsman, sound, sound the
 gay horn,
  Till Phœbus awakens the day,
And see, now he rises in splendor how bright !
IO Pæan for Phœbus, the god of delight ;
All glorious in beauty, now vanish the night,
  Then mount, boys, to horse, and away.

What raptures can equal the joys of the chace ?
Health, bloom, and contentment appear in each
 face,
And in our swift coursers what beauty and grace,
  While we the fleet stag do pursue ?

At the deep and harmonious cry of the hounds,
Struck by terror, he burfts from the foreft's wide
    bounds,
And though like the lightning he darts o'er the
    grounds,
      Yet ftill boys, we have him in view.

When chac'd till quite fpent, he his life does re-
    fign,
Our victim we'll offer at Bachus's fhrine,
And revel in honour of Nimrod divine,
      That hunter fo mighty of fame :
Our glaffes then charge to our country and king ;
Love and beauty we'll charge to, and jovially
    fing,
Wifhing health and fuccefs till we make the houfe
    ring,
      To all fportfmen and fons of the game!

How imperfect is Expreffion.

How imperfect is expreffion,
  Some emotions to impart ;
When we mean a foft confeffion,
  And yet feek to hide the heart !

When our bofoms, all complying,
  With delicious tumults fwell,
And beat, what broken, fault'ring, dying,
  Language would, but cannot tell !

Deep confusion's rosy terror,
  Quite expressive, paints my cheek;
Ask no more—behold your error—
  Blushes eloquently speak.

What, tho' silent is my anguish,
  Or breath'd only to the air,
Mark my eyes, and as they languish,
  Read what your's have written there.

O that you could once conceive me!
  Once my soul's strong feeling view!
Love has nought more fond, believe me;
  Friendship nothing half so true.

From you I am wild, despairing;
  With you, speechless as I touch;
This is all that bears declaring,
  And, perhaps, declares too much.

As sure as a Gun.

ALL you who wou'd wish to succeed with a lass,
  Learn how the affair's to be done:
For, if you stand fooling, and shy, like an ass,
  You'll lose her, as sure as a gun.

With whining, and sighing, and vows, and all that,
  As far as you please you may run;

She'll hear you, and jeer you, and give you a pat,
   But jilt you as fure as a gun.

To worfhip, and call her bright goddefs, is fine,
   But, mark you the confequence—mum;
The baggage will think herfelf really divine,
   And fcorn you as fure as a gun:

Then be with a maiden, bold, frolic, and ftout,
   And no opportunity fhun;
She'll tell you fhe hates you, and fwear fhe'll cry
   out,
   But mum—fhe's as fure as a gun.

The wand'ring Sailor.

The wand'ring failor ploughs the main,
A competence in life to gain,
Undaunted braves the ftormy feas,
To find, at leaft, content and eafe;
In hopes, when toil and danger's o'er,
To anchor on his native fhore.

When winds blow hard, and mountains roll,
And thunders fhake from pole to pole;
Tho' dreadful waves furrounding foam,
Still flatt'ring fancy wafts him home;
In hopes, when toil and danger's o'er,
To anchor on his native fhore.

When round the bowl the jovial crew
The early ſcenes of youth renew,
Tho each his fav'rite fair will boaſt,
This is the univerſal toaſt—
May we, when toil and danger's o'er,
Caſt anchor on our native ſhore !

Poor Tom.

THEN farewell my trim-built wherry,
   Oars, and coat, and badge, farewell ;
Never more at Chelſea ferry,
   Shall your Thomas take a ſpell.

But to hope and peace a ſtranger,
   In the battle's heat I go;
Where expos'd to ev'ry danger,
   Some friendly ball ſhall lay me low.

Then mayhap when homeward ſteering,
   With the news by meſs-mates come,
Even you the ſtory hearing,
   With a ſigh may cry—Poor Tom !

SONG.   *Poor Soldier.*

SLEEP on, ſleep on, my Kathleen dear,
   May peace poſſeſs thy breaſt ;

Yet doſt thou dream thy true-love's here,
　Depriv'd of peace and reſt.

The birds ſing ſweet, the morning breaks,
　Theſe joys are none to me :
Tho' ſleep is fled, poor Dermot wakes,
　To none but love and thee.

What care we for France or Spain.

LORD, what care we for France or Spain?
　Why, let them rave and bellow :
Since Rodney rules upon the main,
　O! he's a charming fellow.

De Graſſe he crow'd like Gallic cock,
　And made his cannons bellow;
But Rodney hit him ſuch a knock,
　O! he's a charming fellow.

Mynheer he met with, ſome time ſince,
　Which did his honour ſwell-o ;
When Digby with our Royal Prince
　Call'd him a charming fellow.

Our foes he'll trim, where'er he goes,
　Ye bells his glory tell-o ;
France, Spain, and Holland he'll oppoſe,
　O what a charming fellow?

From north to fouth, from eaft to weft,
　　Our enemies he'll quell-o ;
Of all our admirals he's the beft,　.
　　O ! what a charming fellow.

Come, tofs the bumper now around,
　　Let fame her trumpet fwell-o ;
Wherever Rodney's name is found,
　　They'll call him charming fellow.

Britifh Tar.

Thus, thus, my boys, our anchor's weigh'd ;
See Briton's glorious flag difplay'd !
　　Unfurl the fwelling fail !
Sound, found your fhells, ye Tritons found !
Let ever heart with joy rebound !
　　We fcud before the gale.

　　See Neptune quits his wat'ry car,
　　　　Depos'd by Jove's decree,
　　Who hails a free-born Britifh tar,
　　　　The fov'reign of the fea.

Now, now we leave the land behind,
Our loving wives, and fweethearts kind,
　　Perhaps to meet no more !

H

Great George commands ; it muſt be ſo ;
And glory calls ; then let us go !
   Nor ſigh a wiſh for ſhore.
    For Neptune, &c.

A ſail a-head, our decks we clear ;
Our canvas crowd ; the chace we're near ;
   In vain the Frenchman flies.
A broadſide pour'd through clouds of ſmoke,
Our captain roars—My hearts of oak,
   Now draw and board your prize !
    For Neptune, &c.

The ſcuppers run with Gallic gore ;
The white flag ſtruck ; monſieur no more
   Diſputes the Britiſh ſway.
A prize ! we tow her into port,
And hark ! ſalutes from ev'ry fort !
   Huzza ! my ſouls, huzza !
    For Neptune, &c.

The Twins of Latona.

THE twins of Latona ſo kind to my boon,
   Ariſe to partake of the chace ;
And Sol lend a ray to chaſte Dian's fair moon,
   And a ſmile to the ſmiles of her face.

For the fport I delight in, the bright Queen of
　　love
With myrtles my brow fhall adorn,
While Pan breaks his chaunter, and fkulks in the
　　grove,
　　Excell'd by the found of the horn.

The dogs are uncoupl'd, and fweet is their cry,
Yet fweeter the notes of fweet echo's reply;
Hark forward, hark forward, the game is in view,
But love is the game that I wifh to purfue.

The ftag from his chamber of woodbine peeps out,
　　His fentence he hears in the gale;
Yet flies, till entangl'd in fear and in doubt,
　　His courage and conftancy fail.

Surrounded by foes, he prepares for the fray,
　　Defpair taking place of his fear!
With antlers erected a while ftands at bay,
　　Then furrenders his life with a tear.
　　　　The dogs are, &c.

Tally Ho.

Y E fportfmen draw near, and ye fportfwomen too,
　　Who delight in the joys of the field,
Mankind, tho' they blame, are all eager as you,
　　And no one the conteft will yield;

His lordſhip, his worſhip, his honour, his gracc,
   A hunting continually go,
All ranks and degrees are engag'd in the chace,
   With hark forward, huzza! tally ho.

The lawyer wi!l riſe with the firſt in the morn,
   To hunt for a mortgage or deed,
The huſband gets up at the ſound of the horn,
   And rides to the common full ſpeed ;
The patriot is thrown in purſuit of the game,
   The poet too often lies low,
Who, mounted on Pegaſus flies after Fame,
   With hark forward, huzza ! tally ho.

While fearleſs o'er hills, and o'er woodlands we
   ſweep,
   Tho' prudes on our paſtimes may frown,
How oft do they decency's bounds o'erleap,
   And the fences of virtue break down ?
Thus public, or private, for penſion, for place,
   For amuſement, for paſſion, for ſhow,
All ranks and degrees are engag'd in the chace,
   With hark forward, huzza ! tally ho.

The Sailor's Advice.

As you mean to ſet ſail for the land of delight,
And in wedlock's ſoft hammocks to ſwing ev'ry
   night,

H 3

If you hope that your voyage fuccefsful fhould
    prove,
Fill your fails with affection, your cabbins with
    love.
       Fill your fails, &c.

Let your hearts, like your main-maft, be ever up-
    right,
And the union you boaft, like your tackle be tight,
Of the fhoals of indiff'rence be fure you keep clear,
And the quickfands of jealoufy never come near.
       And the quickfands, &c.

If vapours and whims, like fea-ficknefs prevail,
You muft fpread all your canvas, and catch the
    frefh gale ;
But if brifk blows the wind, and there comes a
    rough fea,
Then lower your top-fails, and fcud under lee.
       Then lower, &c.

If hufbands, you hope to live peaceable lives,
Keep the reck'ning yourfelves, give the helm to
    your wives,
For the evener we go, boys, the better we fail,
And on fhipboard the head is ftill rul'd by the tail.
       And on fhipboard, &c.

Then liften to your pilot, my boys, and be wife,
If my precepts you fcorn, and my maxims defpife,

A brace of proud antlers your brows may adorn,
And a hundred to one but you double Cape Horn,
And a hundred, &c.

The happy Soldier.

How happy's the foldier who lives on his pay,
And fpends half-a-crown out of fixpence a-day;
Yet fears neither juftice, warrants, nor bums,
But pays all his debts with the roll of his drum.
With a row-de-dow, &c.

He cares not a marvedy how the world goes,
His king finds him quarters, and money, and
clothes;
He laughs at all forrow whenever it comes,
And rattles away with the roll of the drum.
With a row-de-dow, &c.

The drum is his glory, his joy, and delight,
It leads him to pleafure, as well as to fight;
No girl when fhe hears it, tho' ever fo glum,
But packs up her tatters and follows the drum.
With a row-de-dow, &c.

Balynamono. Ora.

You know I'm your prieft and your confcience is
    mine,
But if you grow wicked, 'tis not a good fign,
So leave off your racking and marry a wife,
And then, my dear Darby, you're fettl'd for life.
      Sing Ballynamono Oro,
      A good merry wedding for me.

The bans being publifh'd, to chapel we go,
The bride and bridegroom in coats white as fnow,
So modeft her air, and fo fheepifh your look,
You out with your ring, and I pull out my book,
      Sing Ballynamono, &c.

I thumb out the place, and I then read away,
He blufhes at love, and fhe whifpers obey,
You take her dear hand to have and to hold,
I fhut up my book, and I pocket your gold.
      Sing Ballynamono, &c.
      That fnug little guinea for me.

The neighbours wifh joy to the bridegroom and
    bride,
The pipers before us march fide by fide ;
A plentiful dinner gives mirth to each face ;
The piper plays up, myfelf I fay the grace.
      Sing Ballynamono, &c.
      A good wedding dinner for me,

The joke now goes round, and the ftocking is
 thrown;
The curtains are drawn, and you're both left a.
 alone;
'Tis then my good boy, I believe you at home,
And hy for a chrift'ning at nine months to come,
  Sing Ballynamono, &c.
  A good merry chrift'ning for me.

Patty Clover.

WHEN little on the village green
 We play'd, I learn'd to love her;
She feem'd to me fome fairy queen,
 So light tripp'd Patty Clover.

With ev'ry fimple childifh art
 I try'd each day to move her;
The cherry pluck'd the bleeding heart,
 To give to Patty Clover.

The faireft flow'rs to deck her breaft,
 I chofe—an infant lover;
I ftole the goldfinch from its neft,
 To give to Patty Clover.

Song.

I sail'd in the good ship Kitty,
  With a ftiff blowing gale and rough fea,
Left Polly the lads call fo pretty,
  Safe here at anchor, yo yea, yo yea, yo yea,
    yo yea, yo yea.
She blubber'd falt tears when we parted,
  And cry'd, now be conftant to me ;
I told her not to be down-hearted,
  So up with the anchor, yo yea.
When the wind whiftl'd larboard and ftarboard,
  And the ftorm came on weather and lee,
The hope I with her fhould be harbour'd,
  Was my cable and anchor, yo yea.
And yet, my boys, would you believe me,
  I return'd with no rhino from fea ;
My Polly wou'd never receive me,
  So again I heav'd anchor, yo yea.

The Bowmen of the Border.

Where Tweed and Teviot ftreams unite,
  And flow in focial order ;
I fing with no unmeaning flight,
  The bowmen of the border.
In Kelfo form'd on focial plan,
The band that rivets man to man,
  Each gallant bowman's enter'd,
Where humour, wit, and fenfe combine,

To lend their aid, with gen'rous wine,
  In these true joys are center'd.
    Long, long renown'd, for fame and skill,
      By Time that old recorder;
    Where Scotia's sons, the foe to kill,
      By bowmen of the border.
Of high renown, in days of yore,
  A noble bowman stood, Sir;
Ulysses, fam'd in classic lore,
  Whose bow no man withstood, Sir:
Fam'd Robin Hood, and little John,
And many a brave and gallant son,
Who drew the twanging yew, Sir;
But Robin Hood, nor little John,
Nor any who the target won,
  Were archers e'er more true, Sir.
      Long, long renown'd, &c.
Nor less to fight their country's cause,
  The band of bowmen came, Sir;
Protectors of its valu'd laws,
  As well as kill the game, Sir,
Oh, let me for a moment dwell,
On that bold archer William Tell*,
  Who gave his country freedom,
And be this theme, our constant toast,
May we an equal virtue boast,
  To use ours when we need 'em.
    Long, long renown'd, for fame and skill,
      The first in martial order,
    Be Scotia's sons, their foe to kill,
      By bowmen of the border.

* The Switser.

The Plough Boy.

A FLAXEN-headed cow boy,
  As fimple as may be,
And next a merry plough boy,
  I whiftled o'er the lea :
But now a faucy footman,
  I ftrut in worfted lace,
And foon I'll be a butler,
  And wag my jolly face.

When fteward I'm promoted,
  I'll fnip a tradefman's bill,
My mafter's coffers empty,
  My pockets for to fill :
When lolling in my chariot,
  So great a man I'll be,
You'll forget the little plough-boy
  That whiftled o'er the lea.

I'll buy votes at elections,
  But when I've made the pelf,
I'll ftand poll for parliament,
  And then vote in myfelf :
Whatever's good for me, Sir,
  I never will oppofe ;
When all my ayes are fold off,
  Why, then I'll fell my noes.

I'll joke, harangue, and paragraph,
  With fpeeches charm the ear,

And when I'm tir'd on my legs,
   Then I'll fit down a peer.
In court or city honour,
   So great a man I'll be,
You'll forget the little plough boy
   That whiftl'd o'er the lea.

The Miller.

MERRY may the maid be
   That marries the miller,
For foul day and fair day
   He's ay bringing till her;
Has ay a penny in his purfe
   For dinner and for fupper:
And gin ye pleafe, a good fat cheefe,
   And lumps of yellow butter.

When Jamie firft did woo me,
   I fpier'd what was his calling;
Fair maid, fays he, O come and fee,
   Ye're welcome to my dwelling:
Though I was fhy, yet I cou'd fpy,
   The truth of what he told me,
And that his houfe was warm and couth,
   And room in it to hold me.

Behind the door a bag of meal,
   And in the kift was plenty;

Of good hard cakes his mither bakes,
　And bannocks were na fcanty;
A good fat fow, and fleeky cow
　Was ftanding in the byre;
Whilft lazy pufs with meally moufe,
　Was playing at the fire.

Good figns are thefe, my mither fays,
　And bids me tak the miller;
For foul day and fair day,
　He's ay bringing till her;
For meal and ma't fhe does na want,
　Nor ony thing that's dainty:
And now and then a keckling hen
　To lay her eggs in plenty.

In winter when the wind and rain
　Blaws o'er the houfe and byre,
He fits befide a clean hearth ftane,
　Before a roufing fire:
With nut-brown ale, he tells his tale,
　Which rows him o'er fou nappy;
Who'd be a king?—a petty thing,
　When a miller lives fo happy.

Totterdown-hill.

AT Totterdown-hill there dwelt an old pair,
　And it may be they dwell there ftill,
Much riches indeed did not fall to their fhare,
　They kept a fmall farm and a mill.

I

But fully content with what they did get,
  They knew not of guile nor of arts ;
One daughter they had, her name it was Bet,
  And fhe was the pride of their hearts.

Nut-brown were her locks, her fhape it was ftraight,
  Her eyes were as black a floe :
Her teeth were milk-white, full fmart was her
    gait,
  And fleek was her fkin as a doe :
All thick were the clouds, and the rain it did pour,
  No bit of blue fky could be fpy'd,
A child, wet and cold, came and knock'd at the
    door,
  Its mam it had loft, and it cry'd.

Young Bet was as mild as the mornings of May,
  The babe fhe hugg'd clofe to her breaft ;
She chaf'd him all o'er, and fmil'd as he lay,
  She kifs'd him and lull'd him to reft ;
But who do you think fhe had got for her prize ?
  Why Love, the fly mafter of arts !
No fooner he wak'd, but he dropp'd his difguife,
  And fhew'd her his wings and his darts.

Quoth he, I am Love ; but, oh, be not afraid,
  Tho' all I may fhake at my will ;
So good and kind have you been, my fair maid,
  No harm fhall you feel from my fkill ;
My mother ne'er dealt with fuch fondnefs by me,
  A friend you fhall find in me ftill ;

Take my quiver and fhoot, be greater than fhe,
The Venus of Totterdown-hill.

Johnny and Mary.

Down the burn, and thro' the mead,
   His golden locks wav'd o'er his brow,
Johnny lilting tun'd his reed,
   And Mary wip'd her bonny mou'.

   Dear fhe loo'd the well known fong,
While her Johnny, blithe and bonny,
Sung her praife the whole day long,
      Down the burn, &c.

Coftly claithes fhe had but few,
   Of rings and jewels nae great ftore,
Her face was fair, her love was true,
   And Johnny wifely wifh'd no more;
Love's the pearl, the fhepherd's prize,
O'er the mountain, near the fountain,
   Love delights the fhepherd's eyes.
      Down the burn, &c.

Gold and title gives not health,
   And Johnny could nae thefe impart;
Youthful Mary's greateft wealth,
   Was ftill her faithful Johnny's heart;
Sweet the joys the lovers find!

Great the treasure, sweet the pleasure
Where the heart is always kind.
    Down the burn, &c.

Last Time I came o'er the Muir.

The last time I came o'er the muir,
    I left my love behind me !
Ye pow'rs ! what pain do I endure,
    When soft ideas mind me ?
Soon as the ruddy morn display'd
    The beaming day ensuing,
I met betimes my lovely maid,
    In fit retreats for wooing.

Beneath the cooling shade we lay,
    Gazing and chastly and sporting ;
We kiss'd and promis'd time away,
    Till night spread her black curtain.
I pitied all beneath the skies,
    Ev'n king's when she was nigh me,
In raptures I beheld her eyes,
    Which could but ill deny me.

Should I be call'd where cannons roar,
    Where mortal steel may wound me,
Or cast upon some foreign shore,
    Where dangers may surround me ;
Yet hopes again to see my love,
    To feast on glowing kisses,

Shall make my care at diftance move,
  In profpect of fuch bliffes.

In all my foul there's not one place
  To let a rival enter;
Since fhe excels in ev'ry grace,
  In her my love fhall center.
Sooner the feas fhall ceafe to flow,
  Their waves the Alps fhall cover,
On Greenland's ice fhall rofes grow,
  Before I ceafe to love her.

The next time I gang oe'r the muir,
  She fhall a lover find me;
And that my faith is firm and pure,
  Tho' I left her behind me:
Then Hymen's facred bands fhall chain
  My heart to her fair bofom;
There, while my being does remain,
  My love more frefh fhall bloffom.

Tweed-fide.

WHAT beauties does Flora difclofe?
  How fweet are her fmiles upon Tweed?
Yet Mary's ftill fweeter than thofe;
  Both nature and fancy exceed.
Nor daify, nor fweet-blufhing rofe,
  Nor all the gay flow'rs of the field,

Nor Tweed gliding gently thro' thofe,
   Such beauty and pleafure does yield.

The warblers are heard in the grove,
   The linnet, the lark, and the thrufh,
The blackbird and fweet cooing dove,
   With mufic enchant ev'ry bufh.
Come, let us go forth to the mead,
   Let us fee how the primrofes fpring ;
We'll lodge in fome village on Tweed,
   And love while the feather'd folks fing.

How does my love pafs the long day ?
   Does Mary not keep a few fheep ?
Do they never carelefsly ftray,
   While happily fhe lies afleep !
Tweed's murmurs fhould lull her to reft ;
   Kind nature indulging my blifs,
To relieve the foft pains of my breaft,
   I'd fteal an ambrofial kifs.

'Tis fhe does the virgins excel,
   No beauty with her may compare ;
Love's graces around her do dwell,
   She's faireft, where thoufands are fair.
Say, charmer, where doth thy flocks ftray ?
   Oh ! tell me at noon where they feed ;
Shall I feek them on fweet winding Tay,
   Or the pleafant banks of the Tweed ?

Song. *Quaker.*

WHILE the lads in the village fhall merrily ah,
  Sound their tabors, I'll lead thee along,
And I will fay unto thee, that merrily ah,
  Thou and I will be the firft in the throng.

Juft then, when the youth who laft year won the
    dow'r,
  And his mate fhall the fports have begun,
When the gay voice of gladnefs refounds from
    its bow'r
And thou long'ft in thy heart to make one,
    While the lads, &c.

Thofe joys that are harmlefs what mortal can blame ?
  'Tis my maxim that youth fhould be free ;
And to prove that my words and my deed are the
    fame,
  Believe thou fhalt prefently fee,
    While the lads, &c.

The Loves of John and Jean.

SING the loves of John and Jean,
  Sing the loves of Jean and John;
John for her would leave a queen,
  Jean, for him, the nobleft don,
    She's his queen,
      He's her don ;

John loves Jean,
And Jean loves John.

Whate'er rejoices happy Jean
Is fure to burft the fides of John,
Does fhe, for grief, look thin and lean,
He inftantly is pale and wan ;
Thin and lean,
Pale and wan,
John loves Jean,
And Jean loves John.

'Twas the lilly hand of Jean
Fill'd the glafs of happy John ;
And, heav'ns ! how joyful was fhe feen
When he was for a licence gone !
Joyful feen,
They'll dance anon,
For John weds Jean,
And Jean weds John.

John has ta'en to wife his Jean,
Jean's become the wife of John,
She no longer is his queen,
He no longer is her don.
No more queen,
No more don ;
John hates Jean,
And Jean hates John.

Whate'er it is that pleafes Jean,
Is certain now to difpleafe John ;

With fcolding they're grown thin and lean,
 With fpleen and fpite they're pale and wan.
  Thin and lean,
   Pale and wan,
  John hates Jean,
   And Jean hates John.

John prays heaven to take his Jean,
 Jean at the devil wifhes John;
He'll dancing on her grave be feen,
 She'll laugh when he is dead and gone,
  They'll gay be feen,
   Dead and gone,
  For John hates Jean,
   And Jean hates John.

Bold Jack.

While up the fhrouds the failor goes,
 Or ventures on the yard,
The landman, who no better knows
 Believes his lot is hard;
  But Jack with fmiles each danger meets,
  Cafts anchor, heaves the log,
  Trims all the fails, belays the fheets,
  And drinks his can of grog.

When mountains high the waves that fwell
 The veffel rudely bear,

Now finking in a hollow dell,
    Now quiv'ring in the air,
        Bold Jack, &c.

When waves 'gainft rocks and quickfands roar,
    You ne'er hear him repine,
Freezing near Greenland's icy fhore,
    Or burning near the line;
        Bold Jack, &c.

If to engage they give the word,
    To quarters all repair,
While fplinter'd mafts go by the board,
    And fhot fing thro' the air,
        Bold Jack, &c.

The poor old Woman of eighty.

How kind and how good of his dear majefty,
    In the midft of his matters fo weighty,
To think of fo lowly a creature as me,
    A poor old woman of eighty.

Were your fparks to come round me, in love with
        each charm,
    Say I have nothing to fay t'ye ;
I can get a young fellow to keep my back warm,
    Tho' a poor old woman of eighty.

John Strong is as comely a lad as you'll fee,
    And one that will ne'er fay nay t'ye ;
I cannot but think what a comfort he'll be
    To me, an old woman of eighty.

Then fear not, ye fair ones, tho' long paft your
      youth,
    You'll have lovers in fcores beg and pray t'ye,
Only think of my fortune, who have but one tooth,
    A poor old woman of eighty.

Poor Yanko.

WHEN Yanko, dear, fight far away,
    Some token kind me fend ;
One branch of olive, for dat fay
    Me wifh de battle end.

The poplar tremble while him go,
    Say of dy life take care,
Me fend no laurel, for me know
    Of dat he find no fhare.

De ivy fay my heart be true,
    Me droop, fay willow tree,
De torn he fay me fick for you,
    De fun-flower, tink of me.

Till laft me go weep wid de pine,
    For fear poor Yanko dead ;

He come, and I de myrtle twine,
In chaplet for him head.

───────────

A Bed of Moss.

A bed of mofs we'll ftraight prepare,
Where near him gently creeping,
We'll pat his cheeks, and ftroke his hair,
And watch him while he's fleeping.

Sweet flowers of every fcent and hue,
Pinks, violets, and rofes,
And blooming hyacinths we'll ftrew,
As fweetly he repofes.

And we'll with fond emotion ftart,
And while, with admiration,
We foftly feel his fluttering heart
Partake its palpitation.

───────────

The Lawyer's Life.

By roguery 'tis true,
I opulent grew,
Juft like any other profeffional finner;
An orphan, d'ye fee,
Would juft wafh down my tea,
And a poor friendlefs widow would ferve me for
dinner.

I was to be fure,
Of the helpless and poor
A guardian appointed to manage the pelf;
And I manag'd it well,
But how—say you—tell?
Why I let them all ftarve to take care of myfelf.

With these tricks I went on,
Till, faith fir, anon,
A parcel of ftupid, mean-fpirited fouls,
As they narrowly watch'd me,
Soon at my tricks catch'd me,
And, in their own words, haul'd me over the coals.

In the pillory, that fate
For rogues foon or late,
I ftood, for the fport of a diffolute mob;
Till my neck mafter Ketch
Was fo eager to ftretch,
That I gave up the thing as a dangerous job.

Now a wolf—from their dams
I fteal plenty of lambs,
Pamper'd high, and well fed—an infatiable glutton,
In much the fame fphere
When a man, I move here,
Make and break laws at pleafure, and kill my own
mutton.

Then fince, for their fport,
No one here moves the court,
Nor am I amenable to an employer,
I fhall for ever prefer,
With your leave, my good fir,
The life of a wolf to the life of a lawyer.

†   K

The Yellow-hair'd Laddie.

In April, when primroses paint the sweet plain,
And summer approaching rejoiceth the swain;
The yellow-hair'd laddie would oftentimes go
To wilds and deep glens where the hawthorn-trees
    grow.

There, under the shade of an old sacred thorn,
With freedom he sung his love's ev'ning and morn;
He sang with so saft and enchanting a sound,
That sylvans and fairies unseen danc'd around.

The shepherd thus sung, Tho' young Maya be fair,
Her beauty is dash'd with a scornfu' proud air;
But Susie was handsome, and sweetly could sing;
Her breath, like the breezes, perfum'd in the
    spring.

That Madie, in all the gay charms of her youth,
Like the moon was inconstant, and never spoke
    truth;
But Susie was faithful, good humour'd, and free,
And fair as the goddess that sprung from the sea.

That mamma's fine daughter, with all her great
    dow'r,
Was awkwardly airy, and frequently four;
Then, sighing, he wish'd, would parents agree,
The witty sweet Susie his mistress might be.

Woman for Man.

Wine, wine we allow the brisk fountain of mirth,
It frights away care, and gives jollity birth ;
Yet, while we thus freely great Bacchus approve,
Let's pay the glad tribute to Venus and Love ;
For do what you will, nay, or say what you can,
Who loves not a woman, the wretch is not man.

To the charms of the sex, let us cheerful resign
Our youth and our vigour, they're better than wine:
There's merit, I own, in a gay sparkling glass,
But can it compare with a lovely kind lass?
No, it cannot compare, you may say what you can,
Who prefers not a woman, the wretch is not man.

The enchantments of beauty what force can repel?
The eye's pow'rful magic, the bosom's soft swell,
The look so endearing, the kind melting kiss,
The enjoyments of love are all raptures of bliss ;
Then who woman refuses rejects nature's plan,
He may say what he will, but the wretch is no
    man.

May scandal, misfortune, and direful disgrace,
Be the portion of all th' effeminate race ;
Like Britain, what nation on earth can they find
Whose nymphs are so fair, so inviting and kind?
Then who woman refuses rejects nature's plan,
May they suffer like brutes, nor be pity'd by man.

From a ſtriking example my moral ſhall ſpring,
Who'd act like a man, let him copy his king ;
Like George in his youth, the gay ſpring-tide of
     life,
Let every good fellow now take him a wife.
When by Hymen you're bleſs'd, reſt ſecurely, for
     then
You'll have nothing to do but to prove yourſelves
     men.

'Tis a Huſband I mean.

When firſt a maid within her breaſt,
    Perceives the ſubtile flame,
She finds a ſomething break her reſt,
    Yet knows not whence it came.
       A huſband 'tis ſhe wants.

Now riper grown, at ſight of man,
    Her ſwelling boſom glows ;
Old maids, may ſay, the ſex trepan,
    But Miſs much better knows.
       A huſband 'tis ſhe wants.

If pale and wan the drooping fair
    Seems ſinking in her grave ;
In vain is medicinal care,
    'Tis this alone can ſave.
       A huſband 'tis I mean.

Let maidens ftale their doctrine preach
　'Gainſt what like us they love;
For, truſt me, they the fame would teach,
　If they the fame could have.
　　　　A huſband 'tis I mean.

Then on, dear girls, and boldly prove
　There's truth in what I ſay:
Let Hymen take the torch of love,
　And gild each happy day.
　　　　A huſband 'tis I mean.

———————

Broom of Cowdenknows.

WHEN ſummer comes, the ſwains on Tweed
　Sing their ſuccefsful loves,
Around the ewes and lambkins feed,
　and muſic fills the groves.

But my lov'd ſong is then the broom
　So fair on Cowdenknows;
For ſure ſo ſweet, ſo ſoft a bloom
　Elſewhere there never grows.

There Colin tun'd his oaten reed,
　and won my yielding heart:
No ſhepherd e'er that dwelt on Tweed
　Cou'd play with half ſuch art.

He fung of Tay, of Forth, and Clyde,
   The hills and dales around,
Of Leaderhaughs and Leaderfide,
   Oh! how I blefs'd the found.

Yet more delightful is the broom,
   So fair on Cowdenknows;
For fure fo frefh, fo bright a bloom
   Elfewhere there never grows.

Not Tiviot braes, fo green and gay,
   May with this broom compare,
Nor Yarrow banks in flow'ry May,
   Nor bufh aboon Traquair.

More pleafing far are Cowdenknows,
   My peaceful happy home,
Where I was won't to milk my ewes
   At e'en among the broom.

Ye pow'rs that haunt the woods and plains
   Where Tweed and Tiviot flows,
Convey me to the beft of fwains,
   And my lov'd Cowdenknows.

Birks of Invermay.

The ſmiling morn, the breathing ſpring,
Invite the tunefu' birds to ſing ;
And while they warble from each ſpray,
Love melts the univerſal lay ;
Let us, Amanda, timely wiſe,
Like them improve the hour that flies,
And in ſaft raptures waſte the day
Amang the birks of Invermay.

For ſoon the winter of the year,
And age, life's winter, will appear ;
At this thy lively bloom will fade,
As that will ſtrip the verdant ſhade ;
Our taſte of pleaſure then is o'er,
The feather'd ſongſters pleaſe no more ;
And when they droop and we decay,
Adieu the birks of Invermay.

The lav'rocks now and lintwhites ſing,
The rocks around wi' echoes ring,
The mavis and the blackbird vie
In tunefu' ſtrains to glad the day ;
The woods now wear their ſummer-ſuits,
To mirth a' nature now invites ;
Let us be blythſome then, and gay,
Amang the birks of Invermay.

Behold, the hills and vales around
With lowing herds and flocks abound ;

The wanton kids and frisking lambs
Gambol and dance about their dams;
The busy bee with humming noise,
And a' the reptile kind rejoice;
Let us like them, then sing and play,
About the birks of Invermay.

Hark, how the waters, as they fa',
Loudly my love to gladness ca';
The wanton waves sport in the beams,
And fishes play throughout the streams;
The circling sun does now advance,
And all the planets round him dance;
Let us as jovial be as they
Amang the birks of Invermay.

_____

Down the Burn, Davie.

WHEN trees did bud, and fields were green,
    and broom bloom'd fair to see;
When Mary was complete fifteen,
    And love laugh'd in her ee':
Blyth Davie's blinks her heart did move
    To speak her mind thus free,
" Gang down the burn, Davie, love,
    " And I will follow thee."

Now Davie did each lad surpass
    That dwelt on this burn-side,

And Mary was the bonnieſt laſs,
　Juſt meet to be a bride ;
Her cheeks were roſie, red, and white,
　Her een were bonny blue :
Her looks were like Aurora bright,
　Her lips like dropping dew.

As down the burn they took their way,
　What tender tales they ſaid !
His cheek to her's he aft did lay,
　And with her boſom play'd ;
Till baith at length impatient grown,
　To be mair fully bleſt,
In yonder vale they lean'd them down ;
　Love only ſaw the reſt.

" What paſs'd, I gueſs, was harmleſs play,
　" And naething ſure unmeet ;
" For ganging hame I heard them ſay,
　" They lik'd a wa'k ſae ſweet :
" And that they aften ſhou'd return
　" Sik pleaſure to renew ;
" Quoth Mary, Love, I like the burn,
　" And ay ſhall follow you."

Ettrick Banks.

On Ettrick banks, in a Summer's night,
　At gloming when the ſheep drave hame,
I met my laſſie braw and tight,
　Come wading barefoot a' her lane :

My heart grew light, I ran, I flang
 My arms about her lily neck,
And kifs'd and clapt her there fou lang,
 My words they were na mony feck.

I faid, my laffie, will ye go
 To the Highland hills, the Erfe to learn!
I'll baith gi' thee a cow and ewe,
 When we come to the brig of Earn.
At Leith auld meal comes in, ne'er fafh,
 An' herrings at the Broomy Law;
Cheer up your heart, my bonny lafs,
 There's gear to win we never faw.

All day when we have wrought enough,
 When winter frofts, and fnaw begin;
Soon as the fun gaes waft the loch,
 At night when ye fit down to fpin,
I'll fcrew my pipes, and play a fpring;
 And thus the weary night we'll end,
Till the tender kid and lamb-time bring
 Our pleafant Summer back again.

Syne when the trees are in their bloom,
 And gowans glent o'er ilka field,
I'll meet my lafs amang the broom,
 And lead you to my Summer fhield.
Then far frae a' their fcornfu din,
 That mak the kindly heart their fport,
We'll laugh, and kifs, and dance, and fing,
 And gar the langeft day feem fhort.

The unhappy Maid.

FAREWELL ye green fields and fweet groves,
  Where Strephon engag'd my poor heart:
Where nightingales warble their throats,
  And nature is drefs'd without art;
No pleafure they now can afford,
  Nor mufic can lull me to reft;
For Strephon proves falfe to his word,
  And Phillis can never be bleft.

Oft times, by the fide of a fpring,
  Where rofes and lilies appear,
Gay Strephen of Phillis would fing,
  For Phillis was all he held dear;
So foon as he found by my eyes
  The paffion that glow'd in my breaft,
He then to my grief and furprife,
  Prov'd all he had faid was a jeft.

Too foon, to my forrow I find
  The beauties alone that will laft
Are thofe that are fix'd in the mind,
  Which envy, nor time, cannot blaft:
Beware then, ye fair, how ye truft
  The fool who to love makes pretence;
For Strephon to me had been juft,
  If nature had bleft him with fenfe.

Nancy and the Miller.

ONE midfummer morning, when nature look'd gay,
The birds full of fong, and the flocks full of play;
When earth feem'd to anfwer the fmiles from a-
    bove,
And all things proclaim'd it a feafon of love;
My mother cry'd, Nancy, come, hafte to the mill,
If the corn be not ground you may fcold if you will.

The freedom to ufe my tongue pleas'd me no
    doubt;
A woman, Alas! would be nothing without:
I went towards the mill without any delay,
And conn'd o'er the words I determin'd to fay,
But when I came near it, I found it ftock ftill,
Blefs my ftars now! cry'd I, huff him rarely I will.

The miller to market that inftant was gone,
The work it was left to the care of his fon:
Now tho' I can fcold as well as any one can,
I thought 'twould be wrong to fcold the young
    man:
I faid, I'm furpris'd you can ufe me fo ill,
I muft have my corn ground, I muft and I will.

Sweet maid, cry'd the youth, the fault is not mine,
No corn in the town I'd grind fooner than thine;
There's none more ready in pleafing the fair,
The mill fhall go merrily round I declare.

But hark how the birds fing, and fee how they
  bill,
I muft have a kifs firft, I muft and I will.

My corn being done, I towards home bent my
  way,
He whifper'd he'd fomething of moment to fay,
Infifted to hand me along the green mead,
And there fwore he lov'd me indeed, and indeed!
And that he'd be conftant and true to me ftill,
And fince that time I've lik'd him, and like him I
  will.

I often fay, Mother, the miller I'll huff.
She laughs and cries, Go, girl, ay, plague him
  enough ;
And fcarce a day paffes, but by her defire,
I get a fly kifs from the youth I admire.
If wedlock he wifhes, his wifh I'l fulfil,
And I'll anfwer, O yes, with a hearty good will.

Kate of Aberdeen.

THE filver moon's enamour'd beam
 Steals foftly through the night,
To wanton with the winding ftream,
 And kifs reflecting light :

L

To courts be gone, heart-foothing fleep,
 Where you've fo feldom been,
While I May's wakeful vigils keep
 With *Kate of Aberdeen.*

The nymphs and fwains expectant wait,
 In primrofe chaplets gay,
Till morn unbars her golden gate,
 And gives the promis'd May;
The nymphs and fwains fhall all declare
 The promis'd May, when feen,
Not half fo fragrant, half fo fair,
 As *Kate of Aberdeen.*

I'll tune my pipe to playful notes,
 And roufe yon nodding grove,
Till new-wak'd birds diftend their throats,
 And hail the maid I love:
At her approach the lark miftakes,
 And quits the new drefs'd green:
Fond birds, 'tis not the morning breaks,
 'Tis *Kate of Aberdeen.*

Now blythfome o'er the dewy mead,
 Where elves difportive play,
The feftal dance young fhepherds lead,
 Or fing their love-tun'd lay.
Till May in morning-robe draws nigh,
 And claims a virgin queen;
The nymphs and fwains exulting cry,
 " Here's *Kate of Aberdeen.*"

Through the Wood, Laddie.

O Sandy! Why leav'ſt thou thy Nelly to mourn!
    Thy preſence could eaſe me,
    When nothing can pleaſe me;
Now dowie I ſigh on the banks of the burn,
Or thro' the wood, laddie, until thou return.

Tho' woods now are bonny, and mornings are
    clear,
    While lav'rocks are ſinging,
    And primroſes ſpringing,
Yet nane of them pleaſes mine eye or mine ear,
When thro' the wood, laddie, ye dinna appear.

That I am forſaken ſome ſpare not to tell,
    I'm faſh'd with their ſcorning,
    Baith ev'ning and morning,
Their jeering gaes aft to my heart wi' a knell,
When thro' the wood, laddie, I wander myſell.

Then ſtay, my dear Sandy, no longer away,
    But quick as an arrow,
    Haſte here to thy marrow,
Wha's living in langour till that happy day,
When thro' the wood, laddie, we'll dance, ſing,
    and play.

Broom of Cowdenknows.

How blithe was I each morn to fee
　　My fwain come o'er the hill!
He leap'd the brook and flew to me;
　　I met him with good will.
　　　　Oh! the broom, the bonny broom,
　　　　　Where loft was my repofe;
　　　　I wifh I were with my dear fwain,
　　　　　With his pipe and my ewes.

I neither wanted ewe nor lamb,
　　When his flocks near me lay;
He gather'd in my fheep at night,
　　And cheer'd me all the day.
　　　　　　　　Oh! the broom, &c.

He tun'd his pipe and reed fo fweet,
　　The birds ftood lift'ning by;
The fleecy flock ftood ftill and gaz'd,
　　Charm'd with his melody.
　　　　　　　　Oh! the broom, &c.

While thus we fpent our time, by turns,
　　Betwixt our flocks and play,
I envy'd not the faireft dame,
　　Tho' e'er fo rich and gay.
　　　　　　　　Oh! the broom, &c.

He did oblige me every hour:
　　Cou'd I but faithful be?

He ftole my heart, could I refufe
  Whate'er he afk'd of me ?
               Oh! the broom, &c.

Hard fate! that I muft banifh'd be,
  Gang heavily and mourn,
Becaufe I lov'd the kindeft fwain,
  That ever yet was born.
               Oh! the broom, &c.

When War's Alarms.

WHEN wars alarms intic'd my Willy from me,
  My poor heart with grief did figh,
Each fond remembrance brought frefh forrow on
    me,
  'Woke e'er yet the morn was nigh.
      No other could delight him ;
      Ah! why did I ere flight him !
Coldly anfw'ring his fond tale,
  Which drove him far, amid the rage of war,
And left filly me thus to bewail.

But I no longer, tho' a maid forfaken,
  Thus will mourn like yonder dove,
For ere the lark to-morrow fhalt awaken,
  I will feek my abfent love,
      The hoftile country over,
      I'll fly to feek my lover,

Scorning ev'ry threat'ning fear,
  Nor diftant fhore, nor cannons roar,
Shall longer keep me from my dear.

Amynta.

My fheep I neglected, I loft my fheep-hook,
And all the gay haunts of my youth I forfook;
Nae mair for Amynta frefh garlands I wove,
For ambition I faid, would foon cure me of love.
  O what had my youth with ambition to do?
  Why left I Amynta? why broke I my vow?
  O gi' me my fheep, and my fheep-hook reftore,
  I'll wander frae love and Amynta no more.

Thro' regions remote in vain do I rove,
And bid the wide ocean fecure me from love!
O fool to imagine that ought can fubdue
A love fo well-founded, a paffion fo true.
            O what had my youth, &c.

Alas! 'tis o'er late at thy fate to repine;
Poor fhepherd, Amynta nae mair can be thine:
Thy tears are a' fruitlefs, thy wifhes are vain,
The moments neglected return nae again.

  O what had my youth with ambition to do?
  Why left I Amynta? why broke I my vow?
  O gi' me my fheep, and my fheep-hook reftore,
  I'll wander frae love and Amynta no more.

Braes of Ballenden.

BENEATH a green fhade, a lovely young fwain
One ev'ning reclin'd, to difcover his pain;
So fad yet fo fweetly he warbled his woe,
The wind ceas'd to breathe, and the fountains to
    flow;
Rude winds, wi' compaffion, cou'd hear him com-
    plain,
Yet Chloe, lefs gentle, was deaf to his ftrain.

How happy, he cry'd, my moments once flew,
E'er Chloe's bright charms firft flafh'd in my view;
Thofe eyes then, wi' pleafure, the dawn could
    furvey,
Nor fmil'd the fair morning, mair chearfu' than
    they;
Now fcenes of diftrefs pleafe only my fight,
I'm tortur'd in pleafure, and languifh in light.

Thro' changes, in vain, relief I purfue,
All, all but confpire my griefs to renew;
From funfhine to zephyrs and fhades we repair,
To funfhine we fly from too piercing an air:
But love's ardent fever burns always the fame;
No winter can cool it, no fummer inflame.

But fee the pale moon, all clouded, retires,
The breezes grow cool, not Strephon's defires:

I fly from the dangers of tempeſt and wind,
Yet nouriſh the madneſs that preys on my mind;
Ah, wretch! how can life be worthy thy care?
To lengthen its moments but lengthens deſpair.

Highland Queen.

No more my ſong ſhall be, ye ſwains,
Of purling ſtreams, or flow'ry plains;
More pleaſing beauties me inſpire,
And Phœbus tunes the warbling lyre;
Divinely aided, thus I mean
To celebrate my Highland Queen.

In her ſweet innocence you'll find,
With freedom, truth, and beauty join'd;
From pride and affectation free,
Alike ſhe ſmiles on you and me.
The brighteſt nymph that trips the green,
I do pronounce my Highland Queen.

No ſordid wiſh, or trifling joy,
Her ſettled calm of mind deſtroy;
Strict honour fills her ſpotleſs ſoul,
And adds a luſtre to the whole;
A matchleſs ſhape, a graceful mein.
All centre in my Higland Queen.

How bleft that youth, whom gentle fate
Has deftin'd for fo fair a mate !
Has all thefe wond'rous gifts in ftore,
And each returning day brings more ;
No youth fo happy can be feen,
Poffeffing thee, my Highland Queen.

———————

The echoing Horn.

THE echoing horn calls the fportfmen abroad,
   To horfe, my brave boys, and away ;
The morning is up, and the cry of the hounds
   Upbraids our too tedious delay.
What pleafure we find in purfuing the fox!
   O'er hill and o'er valley he flies :
Then follow, we'll foon overtake him, huzza !
   The traitor is feiz'd on and dies.

Triumphant returning at night with the fpoil,
   Like Bacchanals fhouting and gay,
How fweet with our bottle and lafs to refrefh,
   And lofe the fatigues of the day !
With fport, love, and wine, fickle fortune defy,
   Dull wifdom all happinefs fours ;
Since life is no more than a paffage at beft,
   Let's ftrew the way over with flow'rs.

Laſt Valentine's Day.

LAST Valentine's day, when bright Phœbus ſhone
   clear,
  had not been a hunting for more than a year,
     Taleo, taleo, &c.
  mounted black Sloven, o'er the road made him
   bound,
  I heard the hounds challenge, and horns
   ſweetly ſound.
     Taleo, taleo, &c.

Hallo, into covert, old Anthony cries ;
No ſooner he ſpoke, but the fox, Sir, he 'ſpies,
     Taleo, &c.
This being the ſignal, he then crack'd his whip,
Taleo was the word, and away he did leap.
     Taleo, &c.

Then up rides Dick Dawſon, who car'd not a
   pin,
He ſprung at the drain, but his horſe tumbl'd in,
     Taleo, &c.
And as he crept out, why, he ſpy'd the old ren,
With his tongue hanging out, ſtealing home to his
   den.
     Taleo, &c.

Our hounds and our horſes were always as good
As ever broke covert, or daſh'd thro' the wood,
     Taleo, &c.

Old Reynard runs hard, but muſt certainly die,
Have at you, old Tony, Dick Dawſon did cry.
   Taleo, &c.

The hounds they had run twenty miles now or
   more,
Old Anthony fretted, he curs'd too and ſwore,
    Taleo, &c.
But Reynard being ſpent, ſoon muſt give up the
   ghoſt,
Which will heighten our joys when we come to
   each toaſt.
    Taleo, &c.

The day's ſport being over, the horns we will
   found,
To the jolly fox-hunters let echo reſound,
    Taleo, &c.
So fill up your glaſſes, and cheerfully drink
To the honeſt true ſportſman who never will
   ſhrink.
    Taleo, &c,

Since Love is the Plan.

Since love is the plan,
  I'll love if I can—
Attend, and I'll tell you what ſort of a man:
   In addreſs how complete,
   And in dreſs ſpruce and neat,
No matter how tall, ſo he's over five feet;

Not dull, nor too witty,
His eyes I'll think pretty,
If fparkling with pleafure whenever we meet.

In a fong bear a bob,
In a glafs a hab-nob,
Yet drink of his reafon his noddle ne'er rob;
Tho, gentle he be,
His man he fhall fee,
Yet never be conquer'd by any but me.
This, this is my fancy;
If fuch a man I can fee,
I'm his, if he's mine; until then, I'll be free.

Tho' Leixlip is proud, &c.

Tho' Leixlip is proud of its clofe fhady bowers,
  Its clear falling waters and murmuring cafcades,
Its groves of fine myrtles, its beds of fweet flowers,
  Its lads fo well drefs'd, and its neat pretty
    maids;
As each his own village muft ftill make the moft
  of,
  In praife of dear Carton, I hope I'm not wrong:
Dear Carton! containing what kingdoms may
  boaft of!
  'Tis Norah, dear Norah! the theme of my
    fong.

Be gentlemen fine, with their fpurs and nice boots
    on,
  Their horfes to ftart on the Curragh of Kil-
    dare;
Or dance at a ball with their Sunday's new fuits
    on,
Lac'd waiftcoaft, white gloves, and their nice
    powder'd hair:
Poor Pat, while fo bleft in his mean humble fta-
    tion,
For gold and for acres he never fhall long;
One fweet fmile can give him the wealth of a
    nation,
From Norah, dear Norah! the theme of my
    fong.

Auld Robin Gray.

WHEN the fheep are in the fauld, and the ky at
    hame,
And a' the warld to fleep were gane,
The waes of my heart fa's in fhowers frae my e'e,
When my guidman lies found by me.

Young Jamie loo'd me well, and he fought me
    for his bride,
But faving a crown, he had naething befide:
To make that crown a pound my Jamie went to
    fea,
And the crown and the pound were baith for me.

M

He hadna been awa' a week but only twa,
When my mither fhe fell ill, and the cow was
    . ftow'n awa';
My father brake his arm, and my Jamie went to
    fea,
And auld Robin Gray came a courting to me.

My father cou'da' work, and my mither cou'dna'
    fpin,
I toil'd day and night, but their bread I cou'dna'
    win;
Auld Robin maintain'd them baith, and, wi' tears
    in his ee',
Said Jenny for their fakes, O marry me.

My heart it faid nay, I look'd for Jamie back,
But the wind it blew high, and the fhip it was a
    wreck,
The fhip it was a wreck, why didna Jenny die?
And why do I live to cry Waes me!

Auld Robin argu'd fair; tho' my mither didna'
    fpeak,
She look'd in my face till my heart was like to
    break:
So they gied him my hand, tho' my heart was in
    the fea,
And auld Robin Gray is a guidman to me.

I hadna' been a wife a week but only four,
When, fitting fae mournfully at the door,

I faw my Jamie's wreath, but I didna' think it
    he,
Till he faid, I'm come back for to marry thee.

O fair did we greet, and muckle did we fay,
We took each but ae kifs, and we tore ourfelves
    away.
I wifh I were dead, but I'm not like to die,
And why do I live to fay Waes me?

I gang like a gaift, and I carena' to fpin,
I darena' think on Jamie, for that would be a fin:
But I'll do my beft a good wife to be,
For auld Robin Gray is kind to me.

The Death of auld Robin Gray, and Jamie's Return.

THE Summer it was fmiling, all nature round
    was gay,
When Jenny was attending on auld Robin
    Gray;
For he was fick at heart, and had nae friend be-
    fide,
But only me, poor Jenny, who newly was his
    bride.

Ah! Jenny, I fhall die, he cry'd, as fure as I had
    birth;
Then fee my poor old banes, I pray, laid into the
    earth;

And be a widow for my fake a twelvemonth and
　　a day,
And I'll leave you whate'er belongs to auld Ro-
　　bin Gray.

I laid poor Robin in the earth as decent as I cou'd,
And fhed a tear upon his grave, for he was very
　　good ;
I took my rock into my hand, and in my cot I
　　figh'd,
Oh, wae's me, what fhall I do, fince poor auld
　　Robin died.

Search ev'ry partthroughout the land, there's nane
　　like me forlorn,
I'm ready e'en to ban the day that ever I was
　　born ;
For Jamie, all I lov'd on earth, Ah ! he is gone
　　away,
My father's dead, my mother's dead, and eke auld
　　Robin Gray.

I rofe up with the morning fun, and fpun till fet-
　　ting day,
And one whole year of widowhood I mourn'd
　　for Robin Gray :
I did the duty of a wife, both kind and conftant
　　too ;
Let ev'ry one example take, and Jenny's plan
　　purfue.

I thought that Jamie he was dead, or he to me
    was loft,
And all my fond and youthful love entirely it was
    croft :
I try'd to fing, I try'd to laugh, and pafs the time
    away,
For I had ne'er a friend alive fince dy'd auld Ro-
    bin Gray.

At length the merry bells rung round, I cou'dna'
    guefs the caufe ;
But Rodney was the man they faid, that gain'd
    fo much applaufe :
I doubted if the tale was true, till Jamie came to me,
And fhow'd a purfe of golden ore, and faid, It is
    for thee ;

Auld Robin Gray, I find is dead, and ftill your
    heart is true,
Then, take me, Jenny, to your arms, and I will
    be fo too.
Mefs John fhall join us at the kirk, and we'll be
    blithe and gay ;
I blufh'd, confented, and reply'd, Adieu to Ro-
    bin Gray.

The Miller's Wedding.

LEAVE, neighbours, your work, and to fport and
  to play;
Let the tabor ftrike up, and the village be gay,
  Let the tabor, &c.

No day thro' the year fhall more cheerful be feen,
For Ralph of the mill marries Sue of the green,
    For Ralph, &c.
  I love Sue, aud Sue love loves me,
    And while the wind blows,
    And while the mill goes,
  Who'll be fo happy, fo happy as we?

Let lords and fine folks, who for wealth take a
  bride,
Be married to-day, and to-morrow be cloy'd;
My body is ftout, and my heart is as found,
And my love, like my courage, will never give
  ground.
    I love Sue, &c.

Let ladies of fafhion the beft jointures wed,
And prudently take the beft bidders to bed;
Such figning and fealing's no part of our blifs,
We fettle our hearts, and we feal with a kifs.
    I love Sue, &c.

Though Ralph is not courtly, nor one of our
    beaus,
Nor bounces, nor flutters, nor wears your fine
    clothes,
In nothing he'll follow from folks of high life,
Nor ne'er turn his back on his friend or his wife.
     I love Sue, &c.

While thus I am able to work at my mill,
While thus thou art kind, and my tongue but lies
    ftill,
Our joys fhall continue, and ever be new,
And none be fo happy as Ralph and his Sue.
     I love Sue, &c.

The happy Pair.

How bleft has my time been ? what joys have I
    known,
Since wedlock's foft bondage made Jeffy my own?
So joyful my heart is, fo eafy my chain,
That freedom is taftelefs, and roving a pain.
     That freedom is taftelefs, &c.

Thro' walks grown with woodbines as often we
    ftray,
Around us our boys and girls frolic and play :
How pleafing their fport is! the wanton ones fee,
And borrow their looks from my Jeffy and me.

To try her sweet temper, oft-times am I seen
In revels all day with the nymphs on the green:
Tho' painful my absence, my doubts she beguiles,
And meets me at night with complacence and
    smiles.

What tho' on her cheek the rose loses its hue,
Her wit and good-humour blooms all the year
    through:
Time still as he flies adds increase to her truth,
And gives to her mind what he steals from her
    youth.
Ye shepherds so gay, who make love to ensnare,
And cheat, with false vows, the too credulous
    fair;
In search of true pleasure, how vainly you roam,
To hold it for life, you must find it at home.

The Linnets.

As bringing home the other day
    Two linnets I had tae'n,
The pretty warblers seem'd to pray
    For liberty again.
Unheedful of their plaintive notes,
    I sang across the mead;
In vain they tun'd their downy throats,
    And flutter'd to be freed.

As passing through the tufted grove
    Near which my cottage stood,

I thought I faw the queen of love
  When Chlora's charms I view'd.
I gaz'd, I lov'd, I prefs'd her ftay
  To hear my tender tale;
But all in vain, fhe fled away,
  Nor could my fighs prevail.

Soon thro' the wound which love had made,
  Came pity to my breaft;
And thus I as compaffion bade,
  The feather'd pair addrefs'd:
" Ye little warblers, cheerful be,
  " Remember not ye flew:
" For I who thought myfelf fo free,
  " Am far more caught than you."

The Wiſh.

When the trees are all bare, not a leaf to be feen,
  And the meadows their beauty have loft;
When nature's difrob'd of her mantle of green,
  And the ftreams are faft bound with the froft:
While the peafant inactive ftands fhiv'riug with
    cold,
  As bleak the winds northerly blow:
When the innocent flocks run for eafe to the fold:
  With their fleeces all cover'd with fnow:

In the yard while the cattle are fodder'd with
    ftraw,
  And fend forth their breath like a ftream!

And the neat-looking dairy-maid fees fhe muft
   thaw
Fleaks of ice which fhe finds in her cream :
When the fweet country maiden, as frefh as the
   rofe,
-As fhe carelefsly trips, often flides,
And the ruftics loud laugh, if by falling fhe fhows
   All the charms that her modefty hides :

When the birds to the barn-door hover for food,
   As with filence they reft on the fpray ;
And the poor tired hare in vain feeks the wood,
   Left her footfteps her caufe fhould betray ;
When the lads and the laffes, in company join'd,
   In a crowd round the embers are met,
Talk of fairies and witches that ride in the wind,
   And of ghofts, till they're all in a fweat :

Heav'n grant in this feafon it may be my lot,
   With the nymph whom I love and admire,
Whilft the icicles hang from the eves of my cot,
   I may thither in fafety retire.
Where in neatnefs and quiet, and free from fur-
   prife,
   We may live and no hardfhips endure,
Nor feel any turbulent paffions arife,
   But fuch as each other may cure.

Bide ye yet.

Gin I had a wee houfe, and a canty wee fire,
A bonny wee wifie to praife and admire,
A bonny wee yardy afide a wee burn,
Farewell to the bodies that yammer and mourn.

And bide ye yet, and bide ye yet,
Ye little ken what may betide ye yet,
Some bonny wee body may be my lot,
And I'll ay be canty wi' thinking o't.

When I gang a-field, and come hame at e'en,
I'll get my wee wifie fou neat and fou clean ;
And a bonny wee bairnie upon her knee,
That will cry pappa or daddy to me.

And bide ye yet, &c.

And if there fhould happen ever to be
A diff'rence a'tween my wee wifie and me,
In hearty good humour altho' fhe be teaz'd,
I'll kifs her and clap her until fhe be pleas'd.

And bide ye yet, and bide ye yet,
Ye little ken what will betide ye yet,
Some bonny wee body may be my lot,
And I'll ay be canty wi' thinking o't.

My Heart's my ain.

'Tis nae very lang finfyne
    That I had a lad o' my ain,
But now he's awa' to anither,
    And left me a' my lane.
The lafs he's courting has filler,
    And I hae nane at a';
And its nought but the love of the tocher
    That's ta'en my lad awa'.

But I'm blyth that my heart's my ain,
    And I'll keep it a' my life,
Until that I meet wi' a lad
    Who has fenfe to wale a good wife.
For tho' I fay't myfelf,
    That fhould na fay't, 'tis true,
The lad that gets me for a wife
    He'll ne'er hae occafion to rue.

I gang fou clean and fou tofh,
    As a' the neighbours can tell,
Tho' I've feldom a gown on my back,
    But fic as I fpin myfel'.
And when I am clad in my curtfy,
    I think myfel' as bra'
As Sufie, wi' a' her pearling,
    That's ta'en my lad away.

But I wifh they were buckl'd together,
    And may they live for life ;

'Tho' Willie does flight me, and's left me,
　　The chield he deferves a good wife.
But, O ! I'm blithe that I've mifs'd him,
　　As blithe as I weel can be ;
For ane that's fae keen o' the filler
　　will ne'er agree wi' me.

But, as the truth is, I'm hearty,
　　I hate to be fcrimpit and fcant :
The wee thing I hae I'll make ufe o't,
　　And nae ane about me fhall want.
For I'm a gude guide o' the warld,
　　I ken when to had and to gie ;
For whinging and cringing for filler
　　Will ne'er agree wi' me.

Contentment is better than riches,
　　An' he wha has that has enough :
The mafter is feldom fo happy
　　As Robin that drives the plough.
But if a young lad would caft up,
　To make me his partner for life,
If the chield has the fenfe to be happy,
　　He'll fa' on his feet for a wife.

He's ftole my tender Heart away.

THE fields were green, the hills were gay,
And birds were finging on each fpray,

† 　　　　　　　N

When Colin met me in the grove,
And told me tender tales of love,
Was ever fwain fo blythe as he,
So kind, fo faithful, and fo free!
In fpite of all my friends could fay,
Young Colin ftole my heart away!
　　In fpite of all, &c.

Whene'er he trips the meads along,
He fweetly joins the woodlark's fong;
And when he dances on the green,
'There's none fo blythe as Colin feen:
If he's but by, I nothing fear,
For I alone am all his care;
Then, in fpite of all my friends can fay,
He's ftole my tender heart away.

My mother chides whene'er I roam,
And feems furpris'd I quit my home;
But fhe'd not wonder that I rove,
Did fhe but feel how much I love:
Full well I know the gen'rous fwain
Will never give my bofom pain;
Then in fpite of all my friends can fay,
He's ftole my tender heart away.

But what is that to you?

My Jeany and I had toil'd
　　The live-lang fummer's day,
Till we were almoft fpoil'd
　　At making of the hay.

Her kerchy was of holland clear,
   Ty'd on her bonny brow;
'I whifper'd fomething in her ear,—
   But what is that to you!
     But what is that, &c.

Her ftockings were of kerfy green,
   As tight as ony filk:
Oh! fic a leg was never feen!
   Her fkin was white as milk!
Her hair was black as ane could wifh,
   And fweet, fweet was her mou'!
Oh! Jeany daintily can kifs!—
   But what is that to you?

The rofe and lily baith combine
   To make my Jeany fair;
There is nae bennifon like mine,
   I have amaift nae care:
But when another fwain, my dear,
   Shall fay you're fair to view,
Let Jeany whifper in his ear,
   Pray what is that to you?

Conceal thy beauties if you can,
   Hide that fweet face of thine,
That I may only be the man
   Enjoys thefe looks divine.
O do not proftitute, my dear,
   Wonders to common view,

And I with faithful heart fhall fwear
 For ever to be true.

King Solomon had wives enew,
 And mony a cuncubine ;
But I enjoy a blifs mair true ;
 His joys were fhort of mine :
And Jenny's happier than they,
 She feldom wants her due :
All debts of love to her I'll pay,
 And what is that to you ?

Social Power.

Come, now, all ye focial powers,
 Shed your infl'ence o'er us ;
Crown with joy the prefent hours,
 Enliven thofe before us :

  Bring the flafk, the mufic bring,
   Joy fhall quickly find us ;
  Sport, and dance, and laugh and fing,
   And caft dull care behind us.

Love, thy godhead I adore,
 Source of gen'rous paffion :
Nor will we ever bow before
 Thofe idols, Wealth or Fafhion.
     Bring the flafk, &c.

Why the plague fhould we be fad,
   Whilft on earth we moulder ;
Rich, or poor, or grave, or mad,
   We ev'ry day grow older.
               Bring the flafk, &c.

Friendfhip ! O thy fmiles divine,
   Bright in ev'ry feature ;
What but friendfhip, love, and wine,
   Can make us happy creatures
               Bring the flafk, &c.

Since the time will fteal away,
   Spite of all our forrow,
Let's be blithe and gay to-day,
   And never mind to-morrow.

      Bring the flafk, the mufic bring,
        Joy fhall quickly find us ;
      Sport, and dance, and laugh, and fing,
        And caft dull care behind us.

The Mind of a Woman can never be known.

THE mind of a woman can never be known,
   You never can guefs it aright :
I'll tell you the reafon, fhe knows not her own,
   She changes fo often ere night.

'Twould puzzle Apollo her whimfies to follow,
 His oracle would be a jeft;
   She'll frown when fhe's kind,
   She'll change with the wind;
And often abufes the man that fhe chufes,
 And him fhe refufes likes beft.

To keep them in temper, I'll tell you the way,
 I'd have you give ear to my plan;
Be merry and cheerful, good-humour'd, and gay,
 And kifs them as oft as you can:
For while you do thefe, you the ladies will pleafe,
 Their affections you're fure for to gain;
   Then be of their mind,
   And quickly you'll find,
'Tis better than wrangling, contending, and jang-
  ling,
 For they'll love you, and kifs you again.

When the Men a courting came.

WHEN the men a courting came,
Flatt'ring with their prittle prattle,
Of their fool'ries I made a game,
Rallied with my tittle tattle.

   Cooing to me, wooing to me,
   Teazing of me, pleafing of me,
   Off'ring pelf, each filly elf
Came cooing, wooing, and bowing to me.

The divine, with looks demure,
   Talk'd of tythes and eating plenty;
Show'd the profits of his cure,
   And vow'd to treat me with each dainty.
            Cooing to me, &c.

The learned ferjeant of the law
   Show'd his parchments, briefs, and papers,
In his deeds I found a flaw,
   So difmifs'd him in the vapours.
            Cooing to me, &c.

Phyfic now difplay'd his wealth,
   With his noftrums; but the fact is,
I refolv'd to keep my health,
   Nor die a martyr to his practice.
            Cooing to me, &c.

But at laft a fwain bow'd low,
   Candid, handfome, tall, and clever,
Squeez'd my hand—I can't tell how,
   But he won my heart for ever.

       Cooing to me, wooing to me,
       Teazing of me, pleafing of me,
       Off'ring pelf, each filly elf,
       I fent all other wooers from me.

My ain kind Deary O.

WILL ye gang o'er the lee-rig,
    My ain kind deary O!
And cuddle there so kindly
    Wi' me, my kind deary O!

At thornie dike, and birken tree,
    We'll daff and ne'er be weary O;
They'll scug ill een frae you and me,
    Mine ain kind deary O!

Nae herds wi' kent or colly there,
    Shall ever come to fear ye O;
But lav'rocks whistling in the air,
    Shall woo like me their deary O!

While others herd their lambs and ewes,
    And toil for warld's gear my jo,
Upon the lee my pleasure grows,
    Wi' you my kind deary O!

One Bottle more.

ASSIST me, ye lads, who have hearts void of guile
To sing in the praise of old Ireland's isle,
Where true hospitality opens the door,
And friendship detains us for one bottle more.
One bottle more, arra', one bottle more,
And friendship detains us for one bottle more.

Old England, your taunts on our country forbear;
With our bulls, and our brogues, we are true and
     fincere,
For if but one bottle remain'd in our ftore,
We have gen'rous hearts to give that bottle more.

In Candy's in Church-ftreet I'll fing of a fet
Of fix Irifh blades who together had met;
Four bottles a-piece made us call for our fcore,
And nothing remained but one bottle more.
Our bill being paid we were loth to depart,
For friendfhip had grappl'd each man by the heart;
Where the leaft touch you know makes an Irifh-
     man roar,   [more.
And the whack from Shilela brought fix bottles

Slow Phœbus had fhone thro' our windows fo bright,
Quite happy to view his bleft children of light;
So we parted with hearts neither forry nor fore,
Refolving next night to drink *twelve* bottles more.

The Mulberry Tree.

BEHOLD this fair goblet was carv'd from the tree,
Which, O my fweet Shakefpeare, was planted by
     thee;
As a relic I kifs it, and bow at thy fhrine,
What comes from thy hand muft be ever divine.
    All fhall yield to the mulberry tree,
        Bend to the,
        Blefs'd mulberry;

Matchlefs was he
That planted thee,
And thou like him, immortal fhall be,

Ye trees of the foreft, fo rampant and high,
Who fpread round your branches, whofe heads
    fweep the fky ;
Ye curious exotics, whom tafte has brought here,
To root out the natives at prices fo dear :
        All fhall yield, &c.

The Oak is held royal, is Britain's great boaft,
Preferv'd once your king, and will always our coaft,
Of the fir we make fhips; there are thoufands that
        fight,
But one, only one, like our Shakefpeare can write,
        All fhall yield, &c.

Let Venus delight in her gay myrtle bowers,
Pomana in fruit-trees, and Flora in flowers ;
The garden of Shakefpeare all fancies will fuit,
With the fweeteft of flowers, and the faireft of
    fruit.
        All fhall yield, &c.

With learning and knowledge the well-letter'd
    birch
Supplies law and phyfic, and graces the church,
But law and the gofpel in Shakefpeare we find,
He gives the beft phyfic for body and mind.
        All fhall yield, &c.

The fame of the patron gives fame to the tree;
From him and his merits this takes its degree;
Give Phœbus and Bacchus their laurel and vine,
The tree of our Shakeſpeare is ſtill more divine.
    All ſhall yield, &c.

As the genius of Shakeſpeare outſhines the bright
    day,
More rapture than wine to the heart can convey,
So the tree which he planted, by making his own,
Has the laurel and bays, and the vine all in one.
    All ſhall yield, &c.

Then each take a relic of this hollow tree,
From folly and faſhion a charm let it be;
Let's fill to the Planter the cup to the brim,
To honour your country do honour to him.
    All ſhall yield to the mulberry tree;
        Bend to thee,
        Bleſs'd mulberry;
        Matchleſs was he
        That planted thee,
    And thou, like him, immortal ſhall be.

My Name is honeſt Harry, O.

My name is honeſt Harry O,
Mary I will marry O;
In ſpite of Nell, or Iſabel,
I'll follow my own vagary O.

With my rigdum jigum airy O,
I love little Mary O,
In fpite of Nell or Ifabel,
I'll follow my own vagary O.

Smart fhe is and bonny O,
Sweet as fugarcandy O,
   Frefh and gay,
   As flow'rs in may,
And I'm her Jack-a-dandy O.
      With my, &c.

Soon to the church I'll have her O.
Where we'll wed together O;
   And that, that done,
   Then we'll have fun,
In fpite of wind and weather O.

With my rigdum jigum airy O,
I love little Mary O;
In fpite of Nell or Ifabel,
I'll follow my own vagary O.

Follow the Hounds in full cry.

The fun from the eaft tips the mountains with gold,
And the meadows all fpangl'd with dew-drops be-
   hold;
The lark's early matins proclaims the new day,
And the horn's cheerful fummons rebukes our
   delay,

With the fports in the field their's no pleafure can
    vie,
While jocund we follow, follow, follow, follow,
Follow, follow, follow, follow, follow, follow,
Follow, follow, follow the hounds in full cry.

Let the drudge of the town make riches his fport,
And the flave of the ftate hunt the fmiles of the
    court ;
Nor care nor ambition our pleafures annoy,
But innocence ftill gives a zeft to our joy.
       With the fports of the field, &c.

Mankind are all hunters in various degree ;
The prieft hunts a living—the lawyer a fee ;
The doctor a patient—the courtier a place,
Tho' often (like us) they're flung out with difgrace.
       With the fports of the field, &c.

The cit hunts a plum—the foldier hunts fame :
The poet a dinner—the patriot a name ;
And the artful coquette, tho' fhe feems to refufe,
Yet in fpite of her airs, fhe her lover purfues.
       With the fports of the field, &c.

Let the bold and bufy hunt glory and wealth,
All the bleffings we afk, is the bleffing of health ;
With hounds and with horns thro' the woodlands
    to roam,
And when tired abroad, find contentment at home.
       With the fports of the field, &c.
          O

Dear Tom, this brown Jug.

DEAR Tom, this brown jug that now foams with
     mild ale,
Out of which I will drink to fweet Kate of the vale,
Was once Toby Fillpot, a thirfty old foul,
As e'er drank a bottle, or fathom'd a bowl ;
In boozing about 'twas his praife to excel,
And among jolly topers he bore off the bell.

It chanc'd, as in dog-days he fat at his eafe,
In his flow'r-woven arbour, as gay as you pleafe,
With a friend and a pipe, puffing forrow away,
And with honeft old ftingo was foaking his clay ;
His breath-doors of lite on a fudden were fhut,
And he dy'd full as big as a Dorchefter but.

His body, when long in the ground it had lain,
And time into clay had diffolv'd it again,
A potter found out, in its covert fo fnug,
And with part of fat Toby he made this brown jug ;
Now facred to friendfhip, to mirth, and mild ale ;
So here's to my lovely fweet Kate of the vale.

Blow high, blow low,

BLOW high, blow low, let tempefts tear the main-
     maft by the board,
My heart with thoughts of thee, my dear, and love
     well-ftor'd,

Shall brave all danger, fcorn all fear,
　The roaring winds, the raging fea ;
In hopes on fhore to be once more
　Safe moor'd with thee.
　　　　　　　　Blow high, &c.

Aloft while mountains high we go,
　The whift'ling wind that fcuds along ;
And the furge roaring from below,
　Shall my fignal be to think on thee,
And this fhall be my fong,
　　　　　　　　Blow high, &c.

And on that night when all the crew,
　The memory of their former lives,
O'er flowing cans of flip renew,
　And drink their fweet-hearts and their wives ;
I'll heave a figh and think on thee,
　And as the fhip rolls thro' the fea,
The burthen of my fong fhall be,
　　　　　　　　Blow high, &c.

Bright Phœbus.

BRIGHT Phœbus has mounted the chariot of day,
And the horns and the hounds call each fportfman
　　　　away ;
Thro' meadows and woods with fpeed now they
　　　　bound,
Whilft health, rofy health, is in exercife found,

Hark away is the word to the found of the horn,
And echo, blithe echo, makes jovial the morn.

Each hill and each valley is lovely to view,
While pufs flies the covert and dogs quick purfue ;
Behold where fhe flies o'er the wide fpreading
    plain,
While the loud opening pack purfue her amain.
        Hark away, &c.

At length pufs is caught, and lies panting for
        breath,
And the fhout of the huntfman's the fignal of
        death,
No joys can delight like the fports of the field,
To hunting all paftime and pleafure muft yield.
        Hark away, &c.

A fweet-fcented Beau.

A fweet-fcented beau, and a fimp'ring young Cit,
An artful Attorney, a Rake, and a Wit,
Set out in a chafe in purfuit of her heart,
Whilft chloe difdainfully laught at their art :
And rouz'd by the hounds to meet the fweet morn,
Tantivy, fhe follow'd the echoing horn.

Wit fwore by his fancy, the Beau by his face,
The Lawyer with Quibble, fet out on the chafe ;

The Cit with exactnefs, made out his account,
The Rake told his conqueft, how vaft the amount!
She laugh'd at their follies and blithe as the morn,
Tantivity, fhe follow'd the echoing horn.

The clamorous noife rous'd a jolly young Swain,
Hark! forward, he cry'd, then bounc'd o'er the
    plain,
He diftanc'd the Wit, the Cit, Quibble, and Beau,
And won the fair Nymph, hollow! hollow!
Now together they fing a fweet hymn to the morn,
Tantivy, they follow the echoing horn.

Balinamone Ora.

WHEREVER I'm going, and all the day long,
Abroad, or at home, or alone in a throng,
I find that my paffion's fo lively and ftrong,
That your name, when I'm filent, runs ftill in my
    fong.
  Sing Balinamone Ora, Balinamone Ora,
  Balinamone Ora, a kifs of your fweet lips for me.

Since the firft time I faw you I took no repofe;
I fleep all the day to forget half my woes:
So hot is the flame in my bofom which glows,
By St. Patrick, I fear it will burn thro' my clothes.
  Sing Balinamone Ora, &c.
  Your pretty black hair for me.

In my confcience I fear I fhall die in my grave,
Unlefs you comply, and poor Phelim will fave,
And grant the petition your lover does crave,
Who never was free till you made him your flave.
    Sing Balinamone Ora, &c.
    Your pretty black eyes for me.

On that happy day, when I make you my bride,
With a fwinging long fword how I'll ftrut and
    I'll ftride,
In a coach aud fix horfes with honey I'll ride,
As before you I walk to the church by your fide.
    Sing Balinamone Ora, Balinamone Ora,
    Your little white fift for me.

The Bonny Sailor.

My bonny failor's won my mind!
    My heart is now with him at fea;
I hope the fummer's weftern breeze
    Will bring him fafely back to me!
I wifh to hear what glorious toils;
    What dangers he has undergone:
What forts he ftorm'd, how great the fpoils
    From France and Spain my failor's won.

A thoufand terrors chill'd my breaft,
    When fancy brought the foe in view;
And day and night I've had no reft,
    Left ev'ry gale a tempeft blew.

Bring, gentle gales, my failor home !
   His fhip at anchor may I fee !
Three years are fure enough to roam ;
   Too long for one that loves like me.

His face by fultry climes is wan,
   His eyes, by watching, fhine lefs bright ;
But ftill I'll own my charming man,
   And run to meet him when in fight.
His honeft heart is what I prize ;
   No weather can make that look old ;
Tho' alter'd were his face and eyes,
   I'll love my jolly failor bold.

Life's Like a Sea, in Conftant Motion.

LIFE's like a fea, in conftant motion,
   Sometimes high and fometimes low ;
Where every one muft brave the ocean,
   Whatfoever winds do blow.
Tho' at night by fqualls or fhowers,
   Or driven by fome gentle gales,
If dangers rife be ever ready
   To manage well the fwelling fails.

What, tho' the wayward winds would blufter,
   Let us not give way to fear ;
But all our patience let us mufter,
   And learn by reafon how to fteer :

Let judgment ever keep us fteady,
  For that's a balance feldom fails ;
If dangers rife, be ever ready
  To manage well the fwelling fails.

Truft not too much your own opinion,
  When the veffel's under way ;
Let good example be your dominion,
  That will feldom lead aftray.
But fhould thunder o'er you fhudder,
  Or Boreas o'er the furface rails,
Let good directions guide the rudder,
  Whilft providence conducts the fails.

When you are fafe from dangers riding,
  In fome favourite port or bay,
Hope be the anchor you confide in,
  Care awhile in flumbers lay ;
Next, each a can of liquor flowing,
  And good fellowfhip prevails ;
Let every heart with rapture glowing,
  Drink, " Succefs unto the Sails !"

The Honey Moon.

Wou'd you know, my good friends, what the ho-
    ney-moon is,
How long the duration, how perfect the blifs,
A proof may be found, and a fample be feen,
In fome boarding-fchool couple juft left Gretna-
    green.

My deareſt, my duck,
My ſweeteſt, my chuck;
Miſs Kitty's an angel, her Billy's a god;
Whips crack, glaſſes jingle,
While ſighs intermingle,
And Cupid aſſents, and goes niddity nod,
Niddity nod, niddity nod,
O'er Kitty the angel, and Billy the god.

Papa's and mamma's ſurly tempers once paſt,
Bright Bloomſbury-ſquare has this couple at laſt
In three week's poſſeſſion, how pleaſures will cloy,
Neglect hurts the lady, and time cools the boy.
So impatient to roam;—
Ma'am you're never at home,
A path ſo vexatious no wife ever trod;
My torment, my curſe;—
You are bad—You are worſe.
While Cupid flies off, from a quarrel ſo odd,
Niddity nod, niddity nod,
And Miſs is no angel, and Billy no god.

To routs hies the lady, to gambling goes maſter,
To part from each other, ne'er couple went faſter,
While raking at night, and diſtraction at noon.
Soon cloſe all the joys of the ſweet honey-moon.
Bleeding hearts, aching heads,
Sep'rate tables and beds,
Render wedlock's ſweet countenance dull as a
clod;

Then hie for a fummons
From grave Doctor Commons,
While proctors and parchments go niddity nod,
Niddity nod, niddity nod,
O'er Kitty the angel, and Billy the god.

Hoot awa, ye Loon.

WHEN weary Sol gang'd down the weft,
And filver Cynthia rofe ;
The flow'r enamell'd banks I preft,
Where chryftal Eden flows.
Young Jockey fat him by my fide,
I kenn'd his meaning foon ;
He afk'd a kifs, I fcornful cry'd,
Ah ! hoot awa, ye loon.

Dear Peggy gin ye flout a youth,
Or gi' that bofom pain,
Which pants wi' honour and wi' truth
To tak thee for its ain ;
Then on his pipe he fweetly play'd,
A maift delightful tune :
But na mair words to him I faid,
Than, " Hoot awa, ye loon.

He faid mefs John fhou'd us unite,
If I to kirk wad gang ;
My bofom beat wi' new delight,
Wi' him I went alang.

The bonny lad I found fincere,
  Not waining like the moon;
So dear I loo'd him, I na mair
  Will " Hoot awa, ye loon."

I Travers'd Judah's barren Sand.

I TRAVERS'D Judah's barren fand,
  At beauty's altar to adore ;
But there the Turks had fpoil'd the land,
  And Sion's daughters were no more.
In Greece the bold imperious mein,
  The wanton look, the leering eye,
Bade love's devotion not be feen
  Where conftancy is never nigh.

From thence to Italy's fair fhore
  I bent my never ceafing way,
And to Loretta's temple bore
  A mind devoted ftill to pray.
But there, too, Superftition's hand
  Had ficklied ev'ry feature o'er,
And made me foon regain the land,
  Where beauty fills the weftern fhore.

Where Hymen with celeftial pow'r
  Connubial tranfport doth adorn ;
Where pureft virtue fports the hour
  That ufhers in each happy morn.
Ye daughters of old Albion's ifle,
  Where'er I go, where'er I ftray,

O charity's fweet children fmile
To cheer a pilgrim on his way.

The Green Sedgy Banks.

On the greenfedgy banks of the fweet winding Tay,
As blithe as the woodlark that carols in May,
I pafs'd the gay moments with joy and delight,
For peace cheer'd the morn, and content crown'd
    the night;
Till love taught young hope my youth to deceive—
What we wifh to be true—love bids us believe.

Wherever I wander, thro' hill, dale or grove,
Young Sandy would follow with foft tales of love;
Enraptur'd he prefs'd me, then vow'd with a figh,
If Jenny was cruel—alas! he muft die;
A youth fo engaging, with eafe might deceive—
What we wifh to be true—love bids us believe.

He ftole my fond heart, then he left me to mourn,
For peace and content, that ne'er can return;
From the clown to the beau the fex are all art,
They complain of the wound, but we feel the fmart:
We join in the fraud, and ourfelves we deceive—
What we wifh to be true—love bids us believe.

Duet.

How fweet in the woodlands, with fleet hound
    and horn
To waken fhrill echo, and tafte the frefh morn;
But hard is the chafe my fond heart muft purfue,
For Daphne, fair Daphne, is loft to my view :—
She's loft !—Fair Daphne is loft to my view.

Affift me, chafte Dian, the nymph to regain,
More wild than the Roebuck, and wing'd with
    difdain;
In pity o'ertake her, who wounds as fhe flies—
Tho' Daphne's purfued— 'tis Myrtillo that dies.—
That dies !—Tho' Daphne's purfu'd, 'tis Myrtillo
    that dies.

Duet.

Time has not thinn'd my flowing hair,
    Nor bent me with his iron hand :
Ah why fo foon the blofom tear,
    Ere autumn yet the fruit demand.

Let me enjoy the cheerful day,
    Till many a year has o'er me roll'd;
Pleas'd, let me trifle life away,
    And fing of love ere I grow old,

P

Duet.

A н ! what avails thy lover's prayer,
　　His incenſe clouds the ſky in vain ;
Nor wealth, nor greatneſs was his care,
　　Thee, thee alone, he begg'd to gain.

With thee to waſte the pleaſing day,
　　When ev'ry hour in joy was paſt ;
With love infenſibly decay,
　　And on thy boſom breathe my laſt.

Logan Braes.

By Logan's ſtreams that runs ſae deep,
Fu' aft wi' gleé I've herded ſheep—
Herded ſheep, or gather'd ſlaes,
Wi' my dear lad on Logan braes.
But, waes my heart theſe days are gane,
And I wi' grief may herd alane,
While my dear lad maun face his faes,
Far, far frae me, or Logan braes.

Nae mair at Logan kirk will he,
Atween the preachings meet wi' me—
Meet wi' me, or when its mirk,
Convoy me hame frae Logan kirk ;
Well may I ſing theſe days are gane,
Frae kirk or fair I come alane ;
While my dear lad maun face his faes,
Far far frae me, or Logan braes.

Jockey is a bonny Lad.

Now Jockey is a bonny lad, a merry lad, a cheery
    lad,
A bonny lad, a canty lad, and juſt the lad for me;
For while he o'er the meadow ſtrays, he's ay ſa
    canty, ay ſa gay,
And aft right happy does he ſay, there's nane he
    loes like me.
    For he's ay kiſſing, ay clapping, ay dawting and
      ſqueezing,
    Ay kiſſing, kiſſing me, he winna let me be.

I met my lad the tither day, friſking o'er a field
    of hay,
Says he, dear laſſie, will you ſtay, and crack a
    while wi' me;
Na Jockey, lad, I dare na ſtay, my minie ſhe'll
    miſs me away,
Then flyte and ſcold a day, an' play the deil wi'
    me.
    But Jockey ſtill continued hugging, tugging,
      dawting, ſqueezing,
    Ay kiſſing, kiſſing, clapping, winna let me be.

Now Jockey ſee my hair's a' down, and ſee you've
    torn a' my gown,
How will I get through the town, come Jockey
    tell to me,

But he ne'er minded what I faid, but wi' my neck
    and bofom play'd,
Though I intreated, beg'd, and pray'd him not to
    tuzzle me.
    But Jockey ftill continu'd hugging, tugging,
      dawting, fqueezing,
    Ay kiffing, kiffing me, till baith down came we.

As breathlefs and fatigu'd I lay, in his arms
    amang the hay,
My blood faft through my veins did play, as he
    lay hugging me ;
I thought my breath would never laft, for Jockey
    danc'd fo devilifh faft,
But what came o'er, I true, at laft, there's deil
    ane kens but me.
    For foon he weary'd o' his dance, and a his
      jumping and his prance,
    And confeft without romance, he was fain to
    let me be.

———————

Skaiting Duet.

This bleak and frofty morning,
All thought of danger fcorning,
This bleak and frofty morning,
All thought of danger fcorning,

Our fpirits brifkly flowing, were all in a glow,
Thro' the fparkling fnow, while a fkaiting we go,
With a fa, la, la, la, la, la, to the found of—
    The merry, merry horn.

From the right to the left we are plying,
Swifter than winds now flying,
    From the right, &c.
In circles we fleep, or poife ftill we keep,
Behold how we fweep, the face of the deep.
With a fa, la, la, la, la, la, la, to the fonnd of—
    The merry, merry horn.

Great Jove looks on us fmiling,
Who thus the time beguiling,
    Great Jove, &c.
Where the waters he feal, ftill rove on our keel,
Our weapons are fteel, and no dangers we feel,
With a fa, la, la, la, la, la, la, to the found of—
    The merry, merry horn.

See, fee our train advances,
See how each fkaiter lances,
Spheres on fpheres furrounding,
Health and ftrength abounding,
The Tritons fhall blow, their conch fhells below,
And their beards fear to fhow, while a fkaiting
    we go,
With a fa, la, la, la, la, la, la, to the found of—
    The merry, merry horn.

Alone by the light of the Moon.

When fairies dance round on the grafs,
   Who revel all night in a roun,'
Then fay, will you meet me, fweet lafs,
   Alone, by the light of the moon?
       Then fay, &c.

Firft fwear you will never deceive
   The lafs you have conquer'd fo foon,
Nor leave a loft maiden to grieve,
   Alone by the light of the moon.
       Nor leave, &c.

I fwear to be conftant and true,
   Nor would I be falfe for a crown:
I'll meet you at twelve on the green,
   Alone by the light of the moon,
       I'll meet, &c.

The nightingale perch'd on the thorn,
   Enchants ev'ry ear with her fong,
And is glad on the abfence of morn,
   To falute the pale light of the moon.
       And is, &c.

How fweet is the jeffamin grove!
   How fweet are the rofes in June!
More fweet is the language of love,
   Breath'd forth by the light of the moon,
       More fweet, &c.

The Sailors wat'ry grave.

WHILE o'er the raging roaring feas,
  The failors heart is fore oppreft,
While landfmen fafe, with health and eafe,
  For wives and children we've no reft ;
To them perhaps ne'er fhall return,
  Our little favings cannot fave,
But we are loft ! and they long mourn,
  The failors cold ! cold ! watry grave.

Kind landfmen, oh ! reflect a while,
  The awful fcenes that us befall,
On failors orphans caft a fmile,
  Poor hearts ! fhou'd they for pity call ;
To them perhaps ne'er to return,
  Our little favings cannot fave,
But we are loft ! and they long mourn,
  The failors cold ! cold ! wat'ry grave.

Contented I am..

CONTENTED I am, and contented I'll be ;
Refolv'd in this life to live happy and free,
With the cares of the world I'm feldom perplex'd,
I'm fometimes uneafy, but never am vex'd ;
Some higher, fome lower, I own there may be,
But there's more who live worfe, than live bet-
    ter than me.

My life is a compound of freedom and eafe;
I go when I will, and return when I pleafe;
I live above envy, alfo above ftrife;
And wifh I had judgment to choofe a good wife;
I'm neither fo low nor fo high in degree,
But ambition and want are both ftrangers to me.

Did you know how delightful my gay hours do pafs,
With my bottle before me, embrac'd by my lafs;
I'm happy while with her, contented alone,
My wine is my kingdom, my cafk is my throne;
My glafs is the fceptre by which I fhall reign,
And my whole privy council's a flafk of champaign.

When money comes in, I live till it's gone;
While I have it, quite happy, contented with none.
If I lofe it at gaming, I think it but lent;
If I fpend it genteelly, I'm always content:
Thus in mirth and good humour my gay hours
      do pafs,
And on Saturday's night I am juft as I was.

The Bagrie O't.

When I think on this warld's pelf,
And how little I hae o't to myfelf;
I figh when I look to my thread-bare coat,
And fhame fa' the geer and the bagrie o't.

Johnny was the lad that held the plough,
But now he has got goud and gear enough;
I weel mind the day when he was nae worth a groat,
And fhame fa' the gear and the bagrie o't.

Jenny was the lafs that mucked the byre,
But now fhe goes in her filken attire :
And fhe was a lafs who wore a plaiding coat,
And fhame fa' the gear and the bagrie o't.

Yet a' this fhall never danton me,
Sae lang's I keep my fancy free :
While I've but a penny to pay t'other pot,
May fhame fa' the gear and the bagrie o't.

———

Dans Votre Lit.

Dans votre lit, my Fanny fay,
When paft the bufy hours of day;
Stay and let me happy be,
To find you fometimes think on me,
                    Dans votre lit.

But whether abfent or in view,
My thoughts are fondly bent on you ;
When in my dreams' I'm full of glee,
And in my arms embracing thee,
                    Dans votre lit.

But foon as dawn appears, my fair,
The blifsful vifion's loft in air ;

Confent and you fhall quickly fee,
'Twill make it fweet reality,
                    Dans votre lit.

The foft confeffion make, my fair,
And with it glad my raptur'd ear;
And in return I'll fwear to thee,
Ten thoufand worlds I'd give to be
                    Dans votre lit.

Nancy of the Dale.

My Nancy leaves the rural train,
    A camp's diftrefs to prove;
All other ills fhe can fuftain,
    But living from her love:
Yet, deareft, tho' your foldier's there,
    Will not your fpirit fail,
To mark the dangers you muft fhare,
    Dear Nancy of the dale?
                    Dear Nancy, &c.

Or fhould you, love, each danger fcorn,
    Ah! how fhall I fecure
Your health—'mid toils which you were borne
    To footh—but not endure:
A thoufand perils I muft view,
    A thoufand ills affail;

Nor muſt I tremble e'en for you,
  Dear Nancy of the dale.
            Dear Nancy, &c.

Plato's Advice.

Says Plato, why ſhould man be vain,
  Since bounteous heav'n hath made him great?
Why looketh he with inſolent diſdain,
  On thoſe undeck'd with wealth or ſtate!
Can coſtly robes, or beds of down,
  Or all the gems that deck the fair;
Can all the glories of a crown,
  Give health or eaſe the brow of care.

The ſcepter'd king, the burthen'd ſlave,
  The humble, and the haughty die;
The rich, the poor, the baſe, the brave,
  In duſt, without diſtinction lie:
Go, ſearch the tombs where monarch's reſt,
  Who once the greateſt titles wore,
Of wealth and glory they're bereft,
  And all their honours are no more.

So flies the meteor thro' the ſkies,
  And ſpreads along a gilded train;
When ſhot—'tis gone—its beauty dies—
  Diſſolves to common air again:

So 'tis with us, my jovial fouls,
  Let friendfhip reign, while here we ftay ;
Let's crown our joys with flowing bowls,
  When Jove commands we muft obey.

——————————

Amo, amas.

Amo amas,
I love a lafs,
As a cedar tall and flender :
  Sweet Cowflip's grace,
  Is her nomn'tive cafe,
And fhe's of the feminine gender.

CHORUS.

Rorum corum,
Sunt divorum,
Divo !——
Tag rag, merry derry, perriwig and hat-band,
Hic, hoc, horum, genativo !

Can I decline,
A nymph divine ?
Her voice like a flute is dulcis ;
  Her oculus bright,
  Her manus white,
And foft, when I tacto, her pulfe is.
        Rorum corum, &c.

Oh my bella,
My puella!
I'll kifs, fecula feculorum:
If I've luck, fir,
She's my uxor;
O dies benidiⅽtorum!
     Rorum corum, &c.

Bufh Aboon Traquair.

HEAR me, ye nymphs, and ev'ry fwain,
  I'll tell how Peggy grieves me;
Though thus I languifh, thus complain,
  Alas! fhe ne'er believes me.
y vows and fighs, like filent air,
  Unheeded never move her.
At the bonny bufh aboon Traquair,
  'Twas there I firft did love her.

That day fhe fmil'd, and made me glad,
  No maid feem'd ever kinder;
I thought myfelf the luckieft lad,
  So fweetly there to find her.
I try'd to footh my am'rous flame,
  In words that I thought tender;
If more there pafs'd I'm not to blame,
  I meant not to offend her.

Yet now fhe fcornful flies the plain,
  The fields we then frequented;

†   Q

If e'er we meet, fhe fhews difdain,
  She looks as ne'er acquainted.
The bonny bufh bloom'd fair in May,
  Its fweets I'll ay remember ;
But now her frowns make it decay,
  It fades as in December.

Ye rural pow'rs, who hear my ftrains,
  Why thus fhould Peggy grieve me ?
Oh ! make her partner in my pains,
  Then let her fmiles relieve me.
If not, my love will turn defpair,
  My paffion nae mair tender ;
I'll leave the bufh aboon Traquair,
  To lonely wilds I'll wander.

Flowers of Edinburgh.

My love was once a bonny lad,
  He was the flower of all his kin,
The abfence of his bonny face
  Has rent my tender heart in twain.
I day nor night find no delight ;
  In filent tears I ftill complain ;
And exclaim 'gainft thofe my rival foes,
  That ha'e ta'en from me my darling fwain.

Defpair and anguifh fills my breaft,
  Since I have loft my blooming rofe ;
I figh and moan while others reft ;
  His abfence yields me no repofe.

To feek my love I'll range and rove,
  Thro' ev'ry grove and diftant plain ;
Thus I'll ne'er ceafe, but fpend my days,
  To hear tidings from my darling fwain.

There's naething ftrange in nature's change,
  Since parent's fhew fuch cruelty ;
They caus'd my love from me to range,
  And knows not to what deftiny.
The pretty kids and tender lambs
  May ceafe to fport upon the plain ;
But I'll mourn and lament in deep difcontent
  For the abfence of my darling fwain.

Kind Neptune, let me thee entreat,
  To fend a fair and pleafant gale ;
Ye dolphins fweet, upon me wait,
  And convey me on your tail ;
Heavens blefs my voyage with fuccefs,
  While croffing of the raging main,
And fend me fafe o'er to that diftant ihore,
  To meet my lovely darling fwain.

All joy and mirth at our return
  Shall then abound from Tweed to Tay ?
The bells fhall ring, and fweet birds fing,
  To grace and crown our nuptial day,
Thus blefs'd wi' charms in my love's arms,
  My heart once more I will regain ;
Then I'll range no more to a diftant fhore,
  But in love will enjoy my darling fwain.

Ah! Chloris. Tune, *Gilderoy.*

AH ! Chloris, could I now but fit
  As unconcern'd as when
Your infant beauty could beget
  No happinefs nor pain.
When I this dawning did admire,
  And prais'd the coming day,
I little thought that rifing fire
  Would take my reft away.

Your charms in harmlefs childhood lay,
  As metals in a mine.
Age from no face takes more away,
  Than youth conceal'd in thine.
But as your charms infenfibly,
  To their perfection preft :
So love as unperceiv'd did fly,
  And center'd in my breaft.

My paffion with your beauty grew,
  While Cupid at my heart,
Still as his mother favour'd you,
  Threw a new flaming dart.
Each gloried in their wanton part :
  To make a lover, he
Employ'd the utmoft of his art;
  To make a beauty, fhe.

Hap me wi' thy Petticoat.

O BELL, thy looks hae kill'd my heart,
 I pafs the day in pain;
When night returns I feel the fmart,
 And wifh for thee in vain.
I'm ftarving cold; while thou art warm;
 Have pity and incline,
And grant me for a hap that charm-
 ing petticoat of thine.

My ravifh'd fancy in amaze
 Still wanders o'er thy charms,
Delufive dreams ten thoufand ways
 Prefent thee to my arms.
But waking think what I endure,
 While cruel you decline
Thofe pleafures, which alone can cure
 This panting breaft of mine.

I faint, I fail, and wildly rove,
 Becaufe you ftill deny
The juft reward that's due to love,
 And let true paffion die.
Oh! turn, and let compaffion feize
 That lovely breaft of thine;
Thy petticoat could give me eafe,
 If thou and it were mine.

Sure Heaven has fitted for delight
 That beauteous form of thine,

Q 3

And thou'rt too good its law to flight,
    By hind'ring the defign;
May all the powers of love agree,
    At length to make thee mine;
Or loofe my chains, and fet me free
    From ev'ry charm of thine.

—————

Lochaber no More.

FAREWELL to Lochaber, and farewell, my Jean,
Where heartfome with thee I have mony day been;
For Lochaber no more, Lochaber no more,
We'll may be return to Lochaber no more.
Thefe tears that I fhed they are a' for my dear,
And no for the dangers attending on weir;
Tho' bore on rough feas to a far bloody fhore,
May be to return to Lochaber no more.

Tho' hurricanes rife, and raife ev'ry wind,
They'll ne'er make a tempeft like that in my mind;
Tho' loudeft of thunder on louder waves roar,
That's naething like leaving my love on the fhore,
To leave thee behind me, my heart is fair pain'd;
By eafe that's inglorious no fame can be gain'd;
And beauty and love's the reward of the brave,
And I maun deferve it before I can crave.

Then glory, my Jeany, maun plead my excufe;
Since honour commands me, how can I refufe?

Without it I ne'er can have merit for thee,
And without thy favour I'd better not be.
I gae then, my lafs, to win honour and fame,
And if I fhould luck to come glorioufly hamc.
I'll bring a heart to thee with love running o'er,
And then I'll leave thee and Lochaber no more.

Peaty's Mill.

THE lafs of Peaty's mill,
  So bonny, blithe, and gay,
In fpite of all my fkill,
  Hath ftole my heart away.
When tedding of the hay
  Bare-headed on.the green,
Love 'midft her locks did play,
  And wanton'd in her een.

Her arms, white, round, and fmooth,
  Breafts rifing in their dawn,
To age it would give youth,
  To prefs 'em with his hand:
Thro' all my fpirits ran
  An extafy of blifs,
When I fuch fweetnefs fand
  Wrapt in a balmy kifs.

Without the help of art,
  Like flowers which grace the wild,
She did her fweets impart,
  Whenc'er fhe fpoke or fmil'd,

Her looks they were fo mild,
  Free from affected pride,
She me to love beguil'd,
  I wifh'd her for my bride.

O had I all the wealth
  Hoptoun's high mountain's fill,
Infur'd long life and health,
  And pleafure at my will;
I'd promife and fulfil,
  That none but bonny fhe,
The lafs of Peaty's mill
  Sou'd fhare the fame with me,

Roflin Caftle.

'Twas in that feafon of the year,
When all things gay and fweet appear,
That Colin, with the morning ray,
Arofe and fung his rural lay.
Of Nanny's charms the fhepherd fung,
The hills and dales with Nanny rung,
While Roflin caftle heard the fwain,
And echo'd back the cheerful ftrain.

Awake, fweet mufe, the breathing fpring
With rapture warms, awake and fing;
Awake, and join the vocal throng,
And hail the morning with a fong;

To Nanny raife the cheerful lay,
O bid her hafte and come away ;
In fweeteft fmiles herfelf adorn,
And add new graces to the morn.

O hark, my love, on every fpray
Each feather'd warbler tunes his lay ;
'Tis beauty fires the ravifh'd throng,
And love infpires the melting fong ;
Then let my ravifh'd notes arife,
For beauty darts from Nanny's eyes,
And love my rifing bofom warms,
And fills my foul with fweet alarms.

O come, my love, thy Colin's lay,
With rapture calls, O come away ;
Come, while the mufe this wreath fhall twine
Around that modeft brow of thine :
O hither hafte, and with thee bring
That beauty, blooming like the fpring,
Thofe graces that divinely fhine,
And charm this ravifh'd heart of mine.

Low down in the Broom.

My daddy is a cankar'd carle,
  He'll nae twin wi' his gear ;
My minny fhe's a fcalding wife,
Had's a' the houfe a-fteer :

But let them fay, or let them do,
    It's a' ane to me :
For he's low down, he's in the broom,
    That's waiting on me.
Waiting on me, my love,   .
    He's waiting on me ;
For he's low down, he's in the broom,
    That's waiting on me.

My aunty Kate fits at her wheel,
    And fair fhe lightlies me ;
But weel ken I it's a' envy,
    For ne'er a jo has fhe.
                But let them, &c.

My coufin Kate was fair beguil'd
    Wi' Johnny i' the glen ;
And ay finfyne fhe cries, Beware
    Of falfe deluding men.
                But let them, &c.

Glied Sandy he came waft ae night,
    And fpier'd when I faw Pate ;
And ay finfyne the neighbours round
    They jeer me air and late.
                But let them, &c.

Now Jenny fhe's gane down the broom,
    And it's to meet wi' Pate ;
But what they faid, or what they did,
    'Tis needlefs to repeat :
                But let them, &c.

But they feem'd blyth and weel content,
  'Sae merry ma't they be ;
For a conftant fwain has Pattie prov'd,
  and nae lefs kind was fhe.

    Ye'ave waited on me, my love,
      Ye'ave waited on me,
    Ye'ave waited lang amang the broom,
      Now I am bound to thee.

    Sae let them fay, or let them do,
      'Tis a' ane to me ;
    For I haye vow'd to love you, lad,
      Until the day I die.

My Jo Janet.

Sweet Sir, for your courtefie,
  When ye come by the Bats then,
For the love ye bear to me,
  Buy me a keeking-glafs then.
Keek into the draw-well, Janet, Janet,
And there ye'll fee your bonny fell, my jo Janet.

Keeking in the draw-well clear,
  What if I fhould fa' in,
Syne a' my kin will fay and fwear,
  I drown'd myfel for fin.
Had the better by the brae, Janet, Janet ;
Had the better by the brae, my jo Janet.

Good Sir, for your courtefie,
   Coming thro' Aberdeen then,
For the love ye bear to me,
   Buy me a pair of fhoon then.
Clout the auld, the new are dear, Janet, Janet;
Ae pair may gain ye ha'f a year, my jo Janet.

But what if dancing on the green,
   And fkipping like a mawkin,
If they fhould fee 'my clouted fhoon,
   Of me they will be tauking.
Dance ay laigh and late at een, Janet, Janet;
Syne a' there faults will no be feen, my jo Janet.

Kind Sir, for your courtefie,
   When ye gae to the crofs then,
For the love ye bear to me,
   Buy me a pacing horfe then.
Pace upo' your fpinning-wheel, Janet, Janet,
Pace upo' your fpinning-wheel, my jo Janet.

My fpinning-wheel is auld and ftiff,
   The rock o't winna ftand, Sir,
To keep the temper-pin in tiff,
   Employs aft my hand, Sir.
Mak the beft o't that ye can, Janet, Janet;
But like it never wale a man, my jo Janet.

Woo'd and married and a'.

Woo'D and married and a',
　Woo'd and married and a',
Was fhe nae very weel aff,
　Was woo'd and married and a'.

The bride came out of the byre,
　And O as fhe dighted her cheeks,
Sirs, I'm to be married the night,
　And has neither blankets nor fheets,
　　Has neither blankets nor fheets,
　　Nor fcarce a coverlet too ;
The bride that has a' to borrow
　Has e'en right meikle ado.
　　　　Woo'd, and married, &c,

Out fpake the bride's father,
　As he came in frae the plough ;
O had your tongue, my doughter,
　And ye's get gear enough ;
The ftirk that ftands i' the tether,
　And our bra' bafin'd'yade,
Will carry ye hame your corn,
　What wad ye be at, ye jad ?
　　　　Woo'd and married, &c.

Out fpake the bride's mither,
　What d---l needs a' this pride ;
I had nae a plack in my pouch,
　That night I was a bride ;

R

My gown was linfy-woolfy,
  And ne'er a fark ava;
And ye hae ribbons and bufkins,
  Mae than ane or twa.
          Woo'd and married, &c.

What's the matter, quo' Willie,
  Tho' we be fcant o' claiths,
We'll creep the nearer the gither,
  And we'll fmore a' the flaes:
Simmer is coming on,
  And we'll get teats of woo;
And we'll get a lafs o' our ain,
  And fhe'll fpin claiths enew.
          Woo'd and married, &c.

Out fpake the bride's brither,
  As he came in wi' the ky;
Poor Willie had ne'er a ta'en ye,
  Had he kent ye as weel as I;
For you're baith proud and faucy,
  And no for a poor man's wife;
Gin I canna get a better,
  Ife ne'er tak ane i' my life.
          Woo'd and married, &c.

Out fpake the bride's fifter,
  As fhe came in frae the byre;
O gin I were but married,
  It's a' that I defire;
But we poor fo'k maun live fingle,
  And do the beft we can;

I dinna care what I fhou'd want,
   If I cou'd get but a man.
          Woo'd and married, &c.

Katty's Anfwer.

My mither's ay glowran o'er me,
   Tho' fhe did the fame before me;
I canna get leave to look on my love,
   Or elfe fhe'll be like to devour me.

Right fain wad I tak ye'r offer,
   Sweet Sir, but I'll tyne my tocher;
Then, Sandy, ye'll fret, and wyte ye're poor Kate,
   Whene'er ye keek in your toom coffer.

For tho' my father has plenty
   Of filler and plenifhing dainty,
Yet he's unco' fweer to twin wi' his gear;
   And fae we had need to be tenty.

Tutor my parents wi' caution,
   Be wylie in ilka motion:
Brag weel o' ye'er land, and there's my leal hand,
   Win them, I'm at your devotion.

We're gaily yet.

WE'RE gayly yet, and we're gayly yet,
And we're no very fou, but we're gayly yet,
Then fit ye a while and tipple a bit,
For we're no very fou, but we're gayly yet.

There was a lad, and they ca'd him Dicky,
He gae me a kifs, and I bit his lippy ;
Then under my apron he fhow'd me a trick ;
And we're no very fou, but we're gayly yet.
And we're gayly yet, &c.

There were three lads, and they were clad,
There were three laffes, and they them had,
Three trees in the orchard are newly fprung,
And we's a' get gear enough, we're but young.

Then up wi't Aillie, Aillie,
Up wi't, Aillie, now,
Then up wi't, Aillie, quo' cummer,
We's a' get roaring fou.

And one was kifs'd in the barn,
Another was kifs'd on the green,
The third behind the peafe ftack,
Till the mow flew up to her een.
Then up wi't, &c.

Now fy, John Thomfon, rin,
Gin ever ye ran in your life ;

De'il get ye, but hey, my dear Jack,
   There's a man got a-bed with your wife.
        Then up wi't, &c.

Then away John Thomſon ran,
   And I trow he ran wi' ſpeed ;
But before he had run his length,
   The falſe loon had done the deed.
        We're gayly yet, &c.

The happy Fellow.

WITH my jug in one hand, and my pipe in the other,
   I'll drink to my neighbour and friend ;
My cares in a whiff of tobacco I'll ſmother,
   Since life I know ſhortly muſt end :
While Ceres moſt kindly refils my brown jug,
   With good ale I'll make myſelf mellow ;
In my old wicker chair I'll ſet myſelf ſnug,
   Like a jolly and true-hearted fellow.

I'll ne'er trouble my head with the cares of the
    nation ;
   I've enough of my own for to mind ;
For the cares of this life are but grief and vexation,
   To death we muſt all be conſign'd :
Then I laugh, drink, and ſmoke, and leave nothing
    to pay,
   But drop like a pear that is mellow;

And when cold in my coffin I'll leave them to fay,
   He's gone, what a hearty good fellow!

Loch-Erock Side.

As I came by Loch-Erock fide,
   The lofty hills furveying,
The water clear, the heather bells
   Their fragrant fweets conveying;
I met unthought my lovely lafs,
   I found her like May morning,
With blufhes fweet and charms fae rare,
   Her perfon all adorning.

Sae kind her looks, how bleft was I,
   When in my arms I clafp'd her,
And fhe her wifhes fcarce conceal'd,
   As fondly I carefs'd her;
She faid, if that ye'll conftant prove,
   And evermore will love me,
I heed not Care's nor Fortune's frown,
   Nor ought but death fhall move me.

But conftant, loving, true and kind,
   For ever you will find me,
And of our meeting here fae fweet,
   Loch-Erock fide fhall mind me.
Inraptur'd then, my lovely maid,
   I cry'd nae mair we'll tarry,
But leave the fweet Loch-Erock fide,
   For lovers foon fhould marry.

The disconsolate Sailor.

WHEN my money was gone which I gain'd in the
 wars,
 And the world 'gan to frown on my fate;
What matter'd my zeal or my honoured scars,
 When indifference stood at each gate.

The face that would smile when my purse was well
 lin'd,
 Show'd a different aspect to me;
And when I could nought but ingratitude find,
 I hi'd once again to the sea.

I thought it unwise to repine at my lot,
 Or to bear with cold looks on the shore;
So I pack'd up the trifling remnants I'd got,
 And a trifle, alas! was my store.

A handkerchief held all the treasure I had,
 Which over my shoulder I threw;
Away then I trudg'd with a heart rather sad,
 To join with some jolly ship's crew.

The sea was less troubled by far than my mind,
 For when the wide main I survey'd,
I could not help thinking the world was unkind,
 And Fortune a slippery jade.

And I vow'd if once I could take her in tow,
 I'd let the ungrateful ones see,

That the turbulent winds and the billows could
    fhow
More kindnefs than they did to me.

The merry Sailor.

How pleafant a failor's life paffes,
  . Who roams o'er the watery main ;
No treafure he ever amaffes,
    But cheerfully fpends all his gain :
We're ftrangers to party and faction,
    To honour and honefty true,
And would not commit a bafe action,
    For power and profit in view.

CHORUS.

Then why fhould we quarrel for riches,
    Or any fuch glittering toys ?
A light heart and a thin pair of breeches,
Goes thro' the world, my brave boys.

The world is a beautiful garden,
  . Enrich'd with the bleffings of life ;
The toiler with plenty rewarding,
    But plenty too often breeds ftrife ;
When terrible tempefts affail us,
    And mountainous billows affright,
No grandeur nor wealth can avail us.
    But fkilful induftry fteers right.
        Then why, &c.

The courtier's more fubject to dangers,
   Who rules at the helm of the ftate ;
Than we, who to politics ftrangers,
   Efcape the fnares laid for the great :
The numerous bleffings of nature,
   In various nations we try ;
No mortals on earth can be greater,
   We merrily live till we die.
            Then why, &c.

The Sailor's Confolation.

JACK was fo comely, fo pleafant, fo jolly,
   Tho' winds blew great guns, ftill he'd whiftle
     and fing ;
Jack lov'd his friends, and was true to his Molly ;
   And if honour gives greatnefs, was great as a
     king.
One night as we drove with two reefs in the
     mainfail,
And the fcud came on low'ring upon a lee-fhore,
Jack went up a loft for to hand the top-ga'ntfail,
A fpray wafh'd him off, and we ne'er faw him more,
     We ne'er faw him more !

CHORUS.

   But grieving's a folly ;
   Come, let us be jolly,
   If we've troubles at fea, boys,
   We've pleafures afhore.

Whiffling Tom ftill of mifchief or fun in the middle,
Thro' life in all weathers at random would jog,
He'd dance, and he'd fing, and he'd play on the
  fiddle,
And fwig with an air his allowance of grog :
Long-fide of a Don, in the Terrible frigate,
As yard arm and yard arm we lay off the fhore,
In and out whiffling Tom did fo caper and jig it,
That his head was fhot off, and we ne'er faw
  him more !
    But grieving's a folly, &c.

Bonny Ben was to each jolly meffmate a brother,
He was manly and honeft, good-natur'd, and free;
If ever one tar was more true than another,
To his friend and his duty, that failor was he :
One day with the david to heave the cadge anchor,
Ben went in a boat, on a bold craggy fhore ;
He overboard tipt, when a fhark and a fpanker
Soon nipt him in two, and we ne'er faw him more.
    But grieving's a folly, &c.

But what of it all, lads, fhall we be down-hearted?
Becaufe that, mayhap, we now take our laft fup;
Life's cable muft one day or other be parted,
And death in faft mooring will bring us all up ;
But 'tis always the way on't, one fcarce finds a
  brother
Fond as pitch, honeft, hearty, and true to the core,
But by battle, or ftorm, or fome d----'d thing or
  other,
He's popp'd off the hooks, and we ne'er fee him
  more.   But grieving's a folly, &c.

The Tar for all Weathers.

I SAIL'D from the Downs in the Nancy,
  My jib, how she smack'd thro' the breeze,
She's a vessel quite rigg'd to my fancy,
  As ever sail'd on the salt seas.
Then adieu to the white cliffs of Britain,
  Our girls and our dear native shore ;
For if some hard rock we shou'd split on,
  We ne'er should see them any more.

CHORUS.

But sailors are born for all weathers,
  Great guns let it blow high, blow low,
Our duty keeps us to our teathers,
  And where the gale drives we must go.

When we enter'd the gut of Gibraltar,
  I verily thought she'd have sunk,
For the wind so began for to alter ;
  She yaul'd just as tho' she was drunk,
The squall tore the mainsail to shivers,
  Helm a-weather, the hoarse boatswain cries ;
Set the foresail a'thwart sea, she quivers,
  As thro' the rough tempest she flies.
                    But sailors, &c.

The storm came on thicker and faster,
  As black then as pitch was the sky ;
But then what a dreadful disaster
  Befel three poor seamen and I ;

Ben Buntlen, Sam Shroud, and Dick Handfail,
　　By a gale that came furious and hard ;
And as we were furling the mainfail,
　　We were every foul fwept from the yard.
　　　　　　　　　　But failors, &c.

Poor Ben, Sam, and Dick cried peccavi,
　　When I at the rifk of my neck,
While in peace they funk down to old Davy,
　　Caught a rope, and fo landed on deck.
Well, what would you have, we were ftranded,
　　And out of a fine jolly crew,
Of three hundred that fail'd, never landed,
　　But I, and I think, twenty-two.
　　　　　　　　　　But failors, &c.

At laft then at fea having mifcarried,
　　Another guefs way fet the wind ;
To England I came and got married,
　　To a lafs that was comely and kind.
But whether for joy or vexation,
　　We know not for what we were born ;
Perhaps we may find a kind ftation,
　　Perhaps we may touch at Cape Horn.
　　　　　　　　　　But failors, &c.

Britannia, or, the Death of Wolfe.

In a mouldering cave, a wretched retreat,
　　Britannia fat wafted with care :

She wept for her Wolfe, then exclaim'd againſt
    Fate,
  And gave herſelf up to deſpair.
The walls of her cell ſhe had ſculptur'd around
  With th' exploits of her fav'rite ſon ;
Nay, ev'n the duſt, as it lay on the ground,
  Was engrav'd with ſome deeds he had done.

The ſire of the Gods, from his chryſtaline throne,
  Beheld the diſconſolate dame,
And, mov'd with her tears, ſent Mercury down,
  And theſe were the tidings that came :
" Britannia forbear, not a ſigh nor a tear,
  For thy Wolfe ſo deſervedly lov'd ;
Thy grief ſhall be chang'd into tumults of joy,
  For Wolfe is not dead, but remov'd.

" The ſons of the earth, the proud giants of old,
  Have fled from their darkſome abodes ;
And, ſuch is the news that in heaven is told,
  They are marching to war with the Gods.
A council was held in the chamber of Jove,
  And this was their final decree ;
That Wolfe ſhould be call'd to the army above,
  And the charge was entruſted to me.

" To the plains of Quebec with the orders I flew,
  Wolfe begg'd for a moment's delay :
He cry'd, " Oh, forbear, let me victory hear,
  " And then the commands I'll obey."
With a dark'ning film I encompaſs'd his eyes,
  And bore him away in an urn ;

S

Left the fondnefs he bore to his own native fhore
  Might tempt him again to return."

Mind, Huffy, what ye do.

When I was of a tender age,
  And in my youthful prime,
My mother often in a rage,
  Cried, girl, take care in time ;
For you're of late fo forward grown,
  The men will you purfue ;
And all day along it was her tone,
  Mind, huffy, what ye do.

CHORUS.

Mind, huffy, what you do, you do,
  Mind, huffy, what you do ;
And all day along it was her tone,
  Mind, huffy, what you do.

Regardlefs of her fond advice,
  I haften'd o'er the plain,
Where I was courted in a trice,
  By each young fylvan fwain :
But, by the by, I do declare,
  A lad I had in view,
Altho' it was my mother's cry,
  Mind, huffy, what you do.
               Mind, huffy, &c.

To Damon, gayeſt of the green,
  I gave my youthful hand,
His blooming face and comely mein,
  I could not well withſtand ;
O then to church we tripp'd away,
  With hearts both light and true ;
And now my mother ceas'd to cry,
  Mind, huſſy, what you do.
                  Mind, huſſy, &c.

Now, ladies all, I pray attend,
  And hence this leſſon learn,
If to your mind a man you find,
  Look not moroſe nor ſtern ;
But take him with a free good will,
  If he's got love for you,
Altho' your mother's crying ſtill,
  Mind, huſſy, what you do.

    Mind, huſſy, what you do,
      Mind, huſſy, what you do, you do,
    Mind, huſſy, what you do ;
      Altho' your mother's crying ſtill,
    Mind, huſſy, what you do.

I'd think on thee, my Love.

IN ſtorms when clouds obſcure the ſky,
And thunders roll, and lightning's fly,

In midſt of all theſe dire alarms,
I think, my Sally, on thy charms.
  The troubled main,
  The wind and rain,
 My ardent paſſion prove,
  Laſh'd to the helm,
  Should ſeas o'erwhelm,
I'd think on thee, my love.

When rocks appear on every ſide,
And art is vain the ſhip to guide,
In varied ſhapes when death appears,
The thoughts of thee my boſom cheers.
    The troubled main, &c,

But ſhou'd the gracious pow'rs be kind,
Diſpel the gloom and ſtill the wind,
And waft me to thy arms once more,
Safe to my long-loſt native ſhore ;
  No more the main,
  I'd tempt again,
 But tender joys improve ;
  I'd then with thee
  Should happy be,
And think on nought but love.

THE END,

CONTENTS.

PAGE

A

A rose tree full in bearing, - - - 48

A tinker I am and my name's Natty Sam, - 62

A plague of these musty old lubbers, - - 64

A voyage over the seas had not enter'd my head, 76

All you who would wish to succeed with a lass, 81

As you mean to set sail for the land of delight 88

A flaxen-headed cow boy, - - 95

At Totterdown Hill there dwelt an old pair, - 97

A bed of moss we'll straight prepare, - - 108

As bringing home the other day, - - 140

Assist me, ye lads, who have hearts void of guile 152

A sweet-scented Beau, and a simp'ring young Cit, 160

Ah! what avails thy lover's prayer, - 170

Amo, amas, - - - - 180

Ah! Chloris, could I now but sit, - - 184

As I came by Loch-Erock side, - - - 198

B

By moon-light on the Green, - - - 52

By the gaily circling glass, - - - 56

By roguery, 'tis true, - - - 108

Beneath a green shade, a lovely young swain, 127

PAGE

Behold this fair goblet, 'twas carv'd from the tree, 153
Blow high, blow low, let tempests tear the main-mast, 158
Bright Phœbus has mounted the chariot of day, 159
By Logan's streams that run sae deep, - - 170

C

Come, come, my jolly lads, - - - 13
Come live with me, and be my love, - 66
Come, now, all ye social powers, . - 148
Contented I am, and contented I'll be, - 175

D

Dear is my little native vale, - - - 49
Down the burn and, thro' the mead, - 99
Dear Tom, this brown jug that now foams with mild ale, 158
Dans votre lit, my Fanny say, - 177

E

Encompass'd in an angel's frame, - 31
Ere bright Rosina met my eyes, - - 72

F

For tenderness fashion'd, in life's early day, 49
Farewell ye green fields and sweet groves, - 119
Farewell to Lochaber, and farewell my Jean, 186

G

Go patter to lubbers and swabs d'ye see, - 5
Gin I had a wee house, and a canty wee fire, 143

H

Hard are the times, is the cry, 'tis no wonder, 27
How blest the maid whose bosom, - 38

PAGE

Happy's the love that meets return, - - 47

Her mouth, with a smile, - - - 52

Had Neptune when first he took charge of the sea, 61

Here's to the maiden of bashful fifteen, - 78

How imperfect is expression, - - 80

How happy's the soldier who lives on his pay, 90

How kind and how good of his dear majesty, 106

How blithe was I each morn to see, - 124

How blest has my time been? what joys have I known 139

How sweet in the woodlands, - - 169

Hear me ye nymphs and ev'ry swain, - 181

How pleasant a sailor's life passes, - - 200

I

I was, d'ye see, a waterman, - - 29

I am a jolly fisherman, - - - 32

In my pleasant native plain, - - 37

I've plenty of lovers that sue me in vain, - 41

I sing the British seaman's praise, - 42

I'm a vot'ry of Bacchus, his godship adore, 45

Jack Rattlin was the ablest seaman, - 66

I sail'd in the good ship Kitty, - - 93

In April when primroses paint the sweet plain, 110

I travers'd Judah's barren sand, - - 167

Jack was so comely, so pleasant, so jolly, 201

I sail'd from the downs in the Nancy, - 203

In a mould'ring cave, a wretched retreat, 204

In storms when clouds obscure the sky. - 207

L

Let care be a ſtranger to each jovial ſoul, - 54

Lord, what care we for France or Spain, - 84

Laſt Valentine's day when Phœbus ſhone clear, 130

Leave neighbours, your work, and to ſport and to play, 138

Life's like a ſea in conſtant motion, - 163

M

Ma chere amie, my charming fair, - 71

Merry may the maid be, - - - 96

My ſheep I negleƈted, I loſt my ſheep-hook, 126

My Jeany and I ha' toil'd, - - 146

My name is honeſt Harry O, - - 155

My bonny ſailor's won my mind, - 162

My Nancy leaves the rural plain, - - 178

My love was once a bonny lad, - - 182

My daddy is a canker'd carle, - - 189

My mither's ay glowran o'er me, - 195

N

No more I'll court the town-bred fair, - 21

No flower that blows is like this roſe, - - 72

No more my ſong ſhall be ye ſwains, - 128

Now Jockey is a bonny lad, a merry lad, - 171

O

On Richmond hill there lives a laſs, - - 15

O ſay, ſimple maid, have you form'd any notion, 77

On Ettrick's banks, in a Summer night, - 117

One midsummer morning when nature look'd gay,   120

O Sandy! why leav'st thou thy Nelly to mourn,   123

On the green sedgy banks of the sweet winding Tay   168

O Bell, thy looks have kill'd my heart,   -   185

R

Returning from the fair one eve,   -   12

S

See the course throng'd with gazers,   -   -   35

Sweet Poll of Plymouth was my dear,   -   67

Some how my spindle I mislaid,   -   -   70

Sleep on, sleep on, my Kathleen dear,   -   83

Sing the loves of John and Jean,   -   103

Since love is the plan,   -   ,   -   131

Says Plato, why should man be vain,   -   179

Sweet Sir, for your courtesie.   -   -   191

T

Tho' Bacchus may boast of his care-killing bowl   7

'Twas in a village near Castlebury,   -   14

To Anacreon in heaven where he sat in full glee,   19

To my muse give attention, and deem it not a mystery 22

The moment Aurora peep'd into my room,   -   25

'Twas in the good ship Rover,   -   -   34

Tho' the fate of battle on to-morrow wait,   -   38

The sun sets in night, and the stars shun the day,   46

The moon had climb'd the highest hill,   -   -   50

The meadows look charming, the birds sweetly sing,   51

PAGE

The wealthy fool with gold in store, - 53

This, this, my lad's a soldier's life, - 63

The topsails shiver in the wind, - - 69

That girl who fain would choose a mate, - 73

The world, my dear Myra, is full of deceit, 75

The blush of Aurora now tinges the morn, - 79

The wand'ring sailor plows the main, - 82

Then farewell my trim-built wherry, - - 83

Thus, thus, my boys the anchor's weigh'd, - 85

The twins of Latona so kind to my boon, - 86

The last time I came o'er the muir, - - 100

The smiling morn, the breathing spring, - 115

The silver moon's enamour'd beam, - 121

The echoing horn calls the sportsmen away, 129

Tho' Lexlip is proud of its close shady bow'rs, 132

The summer it was smiling, all nature round was gay, 135

'Tis nae very lang sinsyne, - - - 144

The fields were green, the hills were gay, 145

The mind of a woman can never be known - 149

The sun from the east tips the mountains with gold, 156

Time has not thinn'd my flowing hair, - 169

This bleak and frosty morning, - - 172

The lass of Peaty's mill, - - 187

'Twas in that season of the year, - 188

U

Up amang yon cliffy rocks, - - - 8

W

When first I ken'd young Sandy's face,   -   10

When the fancy-stirring bowl,   -   -   -   11

When I took my departure from Dublin's sweet town, 16

With a cheerful old friend and a merry old song,   56

When the chill Sirocco blows,   -   -   -   57

When Jove was resolv'd to create the round earth,   58

When Britain first, at heaven's command,   -   59

When it is night and the mid-watch is come,   67

Whilst happy in my native land,   -   -   68

When little on the village green,   -   -   -   92

Where Tweed and Teviot streams unite,   -   93

What beauties does Flora disclose,   -   -   101

While the lads of the village shall merrily ah!   -   103

While up the shrouds the sailor goes,   -   -   105

When Yanko, dear sight far away,   -   107

Wine, wine we allow the brisk fountain of mirth,   111

When first a maid within her breast,   -   112

When summer comes, the swains on Tweed,   113

When trees did bud, and fields were green,   -   116

When wars alarms entic'd my Willy from me,   125

When the sheep were in the fauld and the ky at hame, 133

When the trees were all bare, not a leaf to be seen, 141

When the men a courting came,   -   150

Will ye gang o'er the lee-rig,   -   -   152

Where'er I am going, and all the day long,   161

When weary Sol gang'd down the west,   -   166

PAGE

When fairies dance round on the grafs, - 174
While o'er the raging roaring feas, - - 175
When I think on this warld's pelf, - 176
Woo'd and married and a', - - 193
We're gayly yet, and we're gayly yet, - 196
With my jug in one hand, and my pipe in the other, 197
When my money was gone that I gain'd in the wars, 199
When I was of a tender age, - - 206

Y

You're welcome to Paxton, Robin Adair, 41
Young Jockey he courted fweet Moggy fo fair, 74
Ye fportfmen draw near, and ye fportfwomen too, 87
You know I'm your prieft and your confcience is mine, 91

FINIS.